Cases in Hospitality and Tourism Management

Edited by

Robert M. O'Halloran, Ph.D.
Professor & Director
Kemmons Wilson School of Hospitality & Resort Management
University of Memphis

Ken Jarvis, MBA
Associate Professor
Anne Arundel Community College

Amy Allen-Chabot, Ph.D., R.D.
Associate Professor
Anne Arundel Community College

PEARSON
Prentice
Hall

Upper Saddle River, New Jersey 07458

Library of Congress Cataloging-in-Publication Data

Cases in hospitality and tourism management / edited by Robert M. O'Halloran, Ken
Jarvis, Amy Allen-Chabot.
    p. cm.
    Includes bibliographical references.
    ISBN 0-13-170075-8 (pbk.)
      1. Hospitality industry—Study and teaching—United States. I. O'Halloran, Robert M. II.
Jarvis, Ken. III. Allen-Chabot, Amy.

TX911.5.C37 2006
647.94′071′073—dc22

2004060052

Executive Editor: Vernon R. Anthony
Editorial Assistant: Beth Dyke
Executive Marketing Manager: Ryan DeGrote
Senior Marketing Coordinator: Elizabeth Farrell
Marketing Assistant: Les Roberts
Director of Manufacturing and Production: Bruce Johnson
Managing Editor: Mary Carnis
Production Liaison: Jane Bonnell
Production Editor: Ann Mohan, WordCrafters Editorial Services, Inc.
Manufacturing Manager: Ilene Sanford
Manufacturing Buyer: Cathleen Petersen
Creative Design Director: Cheryl Asherman
Cover Design Coordinator: Miguel Ortiz
Cover Designer: Amy Rosen
Cover Image: Getty Images/Comstock Images
Composition: Pine Tree Composition, Inc.
Printer/Binder: Courier/Stoughton
Cover Printer: Courier/Stoughton

Pearson Education LTD.
Pearson Education Singapore, Pte. Ltd.
Pearson Education Canada, Ltd.
Pearson Education–Japan
Pearson Education Australia PTY, Limited
Pearson Education North Asia Ltd.
Pearson Educación de Mexico, S.A. de C.V.
Pearson Education Malaysia, Pte. Ltd.

10 9 8 7 6 5 4 3 2
ISBN 0-13-170075-8

For information about all Prentice Hall Hospitality Management and Culinary Arts titles visit: www.prenhall.com/pineapple

Contents

Cases in Resort and Club Management 75

Cases in Tourism 93

Introduction

This text provides learning opportunities in hospitality and tourism management through the use of case studies. By studying these cases, you can build on your knowledge, comprehend complex situations, apply theory, analyze situations, create solutions, and evaluate and select outcomes. In the process, you will hone your decision-making skills.

The significance of case studies as learning tools is that there can be many solutions justified by different points of view given similar data and information. Some of the cases in this text provide extensive data; others require assumptions, speculation, and creativity in the decision-making process. It is important to note that it is the thinking and decision-making processes you use that ultimately enhance your learning.

As you read these cases, use the following framework as a guide.

Case Framework for Students

1. *Read the case.*
2. *Identify the relevant content.*
3. *Identify the problem.* Differentiate between symptoms and problems. Is the problem in marketing, human resources, finance, or another area?
4. *Identify the relevant facts.* Which facts are most important for decision making?
5. *Identify assumptions you may be making.*
6. *Generate plausible alternatives for the case.* Should you do nothing? Spend a lot of money to fix the problems? Since neither of these alternatives is typically an acceptable solution, you need to formulate viable alternatives.

7. *Make a decision based on your alternatives.* Decision making requires a balance of information and the ability to evaluate data for its importance. You also need to understand whether the alternatives you have developed are workable. Therefore, a discussion with a faculty member on the decision-making process might be appropriate. A sample decision-making process follows.

Sample Decision-Making Process

1. *Identify the issue.* Is it a well-structured or ill-structured problem? Does it have one solution?
2. *Collect facts and evidence.* What are the facts? Differentiate fact from opinion. Which decision-making tools are needed?
3. *Make judgments and decide alternative results.* Collect new facts. What are the possible outcomes of different judgments?
4. *Identify what role, if any, an individual's experience in the workplace plays in the decision.* Weigh experience in similar situations.
5. *Evaluate the evidence.* Ask the right questions. Decide what criteria are being used to weigh the evidence. Which pieces of evidence will you use to make your decision?
6. *Reach a conclusion (judgment).*

It is critical to identify the type of problem the individuals are facing in a case. Is there one right answer? Next, identify the facts and information that are most relevant to the decision-making process. Not all facts in a case have the same importance. You will decide which evidence or information is most important. The identification of the main issue or problem is a key goal of the case method.

Many cases are ill structured; others may have a preferred solution. Cases may have different orientations. The key issue for some might be marketing; for others it might be communication; while still others might involve organizational behavior, decision making, or supervision. Each case has its own direction, and it should be the facts of that case that determine the direction of the outcome. In the analysis stage of the case process, the reader must be able to identify the most important aspects of the situation given the facts of the case, the problem, and the probable outcome.

An individual's personal experiences and expertise are also involved in this process. Each person is likely to look at the facts of a case differently. Expert opinion can also be helpful in characterizing a situation. If facts in a case indicate that the president of a company or a consultant provided input, then their credibility can influence your decision.

The hospitality and tourism management arena is rich with examples and opportunities for learning. The case studies presented in this text provide a broad spectrum of situations, issues, and learning opportunities from which to select.

Acknowledgments

We thank the following reviewers for their valuable feedback on this book:

Kathleen M. O'Brien, Buffalo State College
Julie Lengfelder, Bowling Green State University

Robert M. O'Halloran
Ken Jarvis
Amy Allen-Chabot

Cases in Food Service Management

MENU EXTENSIONS IN A FAST FOOD OPERATION

THE WAITRESS WITH A NOSE RING

MENU CHANGES RESULTING FROM FOOD DELIVERY
SHORTAGES

THE CASE OF THE EXCESSIVELY BUSY LINE COOK

THE REDESIGN OF A SCHOOL CAFETERIA

THE EMPLOYEE WHOSE PERSONAL HABITS DEFY SANITATION
GUIDELINES

MARKETING INGENUITY AND PRODUCT DEVELOPMENT

VENDING OPPORTUNITIES

THE BUSES ARE COMING! A MANAGEMENT PLANNING CASE
STUDY

REBIDDING THE CONTRACT

Menu Extensions in a Fast Food Operation

Objectives

At the completion of this case study, students should be able to:

1. Assess a menu in terms of the ingredients required.
2. Develop new menu items with minimal expansion of food inventory.

Case Study Narrative

Juanita is the owner of a small fast food restaurant, Fast and Fabulous Burgers, in a midsized town. The restaurant has been open for one year, and sales have been moderately good. The menu for the operation is as follows:

Hamburgers
Cheeseburgers
Chili (ground beef, beans, tomatoes, tomato-based sauce)
French fries
Garden salads with assorted single-serving dressings
Sodas
Iced tea

Condiments and toppings for burgers include:

Lettuce
Tomato

3

Mustard

Mayonnaise

Sour cream (for chili)

Ketchup

Bacon

Relish

Barbeque sauce

Part One

Juanita has a customer comment card on every table and puts a self-addressed card in each drive-through order for one month. The card is 4 by 6 inches and is printed with questions on one side and the address on other side.

Question

1. What questions might be appropriate for the customer comment card? Design a small customer comment card for this operation.

Part Two

After one month, Juanita looks at all the cards and tallies the results. She finds that customers feel the food is excellent and the service is very good. The most common written comment is that more selection is desired. She ponders this and thinks about her limited storage space. She can add some menu items but would like to avoid adding a lot more food items to the inventory.

Question

1. Add three new menu items to this menu while only adding a total of two new inventory items.

Part Three

The second most common comment that Juanita got on the comment card is related to healthier menu items. Patrons stated that they would like some healthier or lower fat and lower calorie items on the menu. Again, Juanita wants to provide customers with the items they desire but does not have the space or desire to add a lot of inventory.

Questions

1. How might you define a *healthy* menu item? Support your definition.
2. Add two new healthy menu items while keeping new inventory items to a minimum.

The Waitress with a Nose Ring

Objectives

At the completion of this case study, students should be able to:

1. Balance humanitarian causes with good business and sanitation principles.
2. Identify some sanitation hazards and take effective steps to eliminate them.
3. Recognize that consumers are concerned about sanitation.

Case Study Narrative

Helen was taking a Saturday afternoon trip to the mall with her young daughter, Isabella, and it was taking longer than expected to get everything done. Her daughter needed to eat soon to prevent a meltdown, so they headed to the food court. This would be fun, a meal alone with her little girl.

They scanned the options. Isabella loves baked potatoes, so they headed over to that vendor. As they approached, Helen was drawn closer and closer in disbelief.

By the time they got to the counter, Isabella had decided on the cheese with broccoli potato; however, Helen already knew that they weren't eating there. You see, as they had been approaching, the employee behind the counter was combing her long black hair with her fingers. She saw Helen and Isabella and approached the counter. As she did this, she adjusted her nose ring.

"Are you ready?" she asked.

"Yes, do you have a comment card?" is all that Helen could manage to say.

"Right there," said the employee as she turned and walked away.

"Mommy, did you order?" asked Isabella.

Now Helen's first problem was to deal with her daughter's hunger and disappointment. She didn't want her to fall apart, so she explained as best she could and talked her into eating somewhere else.

While she was eating, Helen filled out the comment card, which was addressed to corporate headquarters. She wondered whether she needed to go that far; maybe contacting the local manager would be enough. She decided that using the card must be the proper route to take since they were provided. She mailed it in later that day.

About a month later, Helen received a call from the owner of the local franchise. He was genuinely concerned. He revealed to Helen that this particular employee is a troubled teen who he had been trying to give an extra chance. She has since been fired for lack of improvement.

Questions

1. What other ways could have been used by the business owner to give this employee an extra chance?
2. Is the nose ring truly a problem? If so, why?
3. Could you legally deny employment to a person with a nose ring?
4. What other behavior of this employee was undesirable?

Menu Changes Resulting from Food Delivery Shortages

Objectives

At the completion of this case study, students should be able to:

1. Identify the short- and long-term problems associated with shortages of food items at delivery.
2. Recognize the need for record-keeping if food wholesalers are to be held accountable for their actions.
3. Identify the considerations that need to be taken into account when making menu item substitutions.

Case Study Narrative

Jacquey is the owner of a midsized restaurant in downtown Chicago. The restaurant is a medium-priced facility that highlights comfort foods. The restaurant uses six major vendors as follows:

- Produce: Bartlett and Sons Produce Wholesalers
- Staple items: Somerset Food Wholesalers
- Dairy: Klemmer's Dairy Wholesalers
- Meats: Porter's Quality Meats
- Bakery: Brenner's Baked Goods

Other vendors are used as necessary to meet the needs of the facility. The facility uses a just-in-time inventory system since their storage space is limited. Recently Jacquey received a customer review done by a consulting company that sends spotters to restaurants at the request of the manager or owner. These spotters pretend to be customers and then write up their experiences in considerable detail for the owner or manager to review. The spotters' report indicated that when they ordered the fried chicken dinner with cauliflower, they were told by the waiter that the cauliflower was unavailable and that broccoli would be substituted. Jacquey wondered why the facility would run out of cauliflower on that evening and called the head chef to inquire. The head chef, Larry, explained that Bartlett and Sons Produce Wholesalers was out of the item, and there wasn't time to order it from another company. He chose to substitute broccoli for the cauliflower, but this meant that there wasn't enough broccoli for the fried cheese and broccoli bites that are popular appetizers on the menu and have a high gross profit margin. Jacquey asked whether being shorted on items (items ordered but not delivered as requested) was a common problem with the produce company or any other wholesalers. Larry reported that he wasn't sure whether the shortage rate was unusually high but that it does happen on occasion. He went on to say that he didn't think that there were as many shortages last year, when they were using Sutton Produce Wholesalers. Jacquey then asked why the broccoli was used as a substitute. Larry responded that most individuals who like cauliflower also like broccoli so it seemed to make sense at the time. He went on to explain that he didn't realize the cauliflower was missing from the order until the dinner meal production had begun, so he couldn't order extra broccoli to cover both menu needs.

To prevent having to make substitutions in the future, Jacquey recommended that Larry order the frozen version of the major vegetables and keep them on hand for just such a situation. Larry reluctantly agreed but pointed out that shortages are not always in the produce area and that just last week Somerset Food Wholesalers shorted them on cornmeal, resulting in no cornbread for the menu for two days. Jacquey considered talking to the wholesalers in general to stress the importance of filling orders without shortages or substitutions but wasn't sure exactly what she should say.

Questions

1. Was broccoli a good choice as a substitution for cauliflower on this menu? Why or why not?
2. How might the handling of this specific food item shortage be improved?
3. What are the pros and cons of ordering frozen vegetables as a backup in case fresh items are not available?
4. What should Jacquey say to the wholesalers, if anything, regarding shortages?
5. What should Jacquey do to determine whether the shortage rate really is unacceptable and, if it is, how could she reduce the shortage rate?

The Case of the Excessively Busy Line Cook

Objectives

At the completion of this case study, students should be able to:

1. Define several important food service terms and expressions.
2. Describe the importance of sticking with a proven formula for success, whether that is menu, service, training, atmosphere, or another element within the food service establishment.
3. Look for creative solutions to seemingly unworkable issues using analytical thought processes.

Case Study Narrative

Macy's Diner & Delicatessen is a restaurant located in Oakville, Ontario, Canada. The restaurant is situated on Lakeshore Boulevard, a busy four-lane street that still has room for more commercial development. In fact, a large super-hardware store is currently being built across the street from the 160-seat restaurant.

Macy's was recently sold and is now under new ownership. The couple who bought the restaurant are a husband and wife restaurateur team that have owned and successfully run restaurants in Mississauga (a neighboring city) for more than twenty-five years. Since purchasing Macy's, they have remodeled the interior of the restaurant and changed the menu. The new bill of fare offers a variety of comfort foods that have lured Mississauga residents for years.

Since they took the restaurant over, customers have been complimenting the couple on their savory dishes that previously made them famous. Authentic Montreal smoked meat brisket deli sandwiches, homemade soups, fresh salads,

10

daily specials, and a variety of other comfort foods have taken Oakville by storm. The number of staff members had to increase in both the front and back of the house to meet customer demand. Deliveries have also started to constitute a significant revenue stream. Many of the people working in the small businesses that have recently opened next to the super-hardware store have become loyal customers.

As a result, Monday to Friday during the lunch hours of 12:00 P.M. and 2:00 P.M., the restaurant has a line of at least ten people waiting at the front door for a vacant table. These are the types of problems any food service establishment owner would like to have.

Of more concern is the division of labor among the line cooks. One of the three line cooks at Macy's is overly busy during the lunch period. A large steamer next to the cook keeps the smoked meat hot. The cook takes the brisket and places it on a large automatic slicer. The slicer cuts the meat paper-thin, and the same cook then places it on rye or uses it for the other dishes. The cook next to him is not as busy, and the third cook has little to do much of the time.

The famous Montreal smoked meat brisket on rye is the most popular menu item. The smoked meat sandwich can represent roughly 50 percent of the lunch orders on a given day. Other dishes also incorporate the smoked meat, such as the club sandwich style dishes, smoked meat pizza, and smoked meat o'top spaghetti.

There is no room for another slicer in the kitchen, and to put one in the preparation area is not an option. No amount of preparation or prepreparation can improve the situation. To make matters worse, the cooks are beginning to quarrel because of the inequitable workloads during lunch.

Questions

1. What should be done in the short-term to alleviate the growing hostility among the three cooks?
2. To whom should the restaurateur go for help in gathering possible solutions to the lopsided workload situation?
3. What are some possible options for shifting some of the workload from the first cook to the other two cooks?

The Redesign
of a School Cafeteria

Objectives

At the completion of this case study, students should be able to:

1. Analyze a food service environment for potential change.
2. Identify stakeholders in the market.
3. Identify operational issues that need to be dealt with.
4. Recommend viable alternatives for potential implementation in the redesign of a cafeteria.

Case Study Narrative

The challenge for East High School was to create a competitive eating establishment within the school and to increase lunch participation while combating a poor reputation. The purpose of the project was to determine customer needs and demands for food service facilities, and to make the East High School cafeteria a more desirable lunch place for students, teachers, and administrative staff. Numerically, the goal of the renovation project was for customer participation to increase by 400 percent. The benefits of this program also include realizing increased revenues and profits for Public School Foodservice.

Comparable Efforts

If a school food service facility was not designed to meet the needs of the operation, it may not be efficient or economical (Richardson et al. 1990). Students use the food service facilities more than any other support services in the school

(Richardson et al. 1990). This was the situation of most public school food service establishments working to compete with commercial limited service restaurants. To attract customers to the school cafeteria, operators must serve food items that are pleasing to students (Tsakalos and Joynt 1994). Traditional cafeteria designs may work in some instances, but may limit themselves in terms of innovations. For example, in one school, changing the high school cafeteria into a food court scramble system, allowed different areas of the cafeteria to focus on different types of food such as burgers and fries, pizza, salads, sandwiches and salads, and, of course, comfort foods such as turkey and mashed potatoes. This system features food to go for students who like to eat off campus and no lines (Tsakalos and Joynt. 1994).

Each situation will be different and no two cafeterias will look alike because the markets they serve will be different and decisions need to be made based on market analysis. Once the appropriate data has been collected, the interpretation process must begin and decisions made to meet the concerns and needs expressed by all those involved.

Methodology for researching this project included secondary data collection using school records; a survey for faculty and staff; interviews and surveys with students, staff, faculty, administrators, and competitors; focus groups with students and faculty; and qualitative observations of the existing cafeteria facility. In the study students were asked to rate the five components that create and influence their preferred dining choices and food choices. An 82 percent response rate, using a sample of 400 students, was achieved. The sample was selected to provide representation from each grade and include students from each group, (free lunch students and those students not eligible for free lunch). Eighty-three teachers were also sent a survey, and twenty-four responded. This study did not examine budget guidelines and financial statements or consider budgetary limitations.

East High School Facts

Student enrollment at East High School at the time of the study was 1,408. Only 5 percent of the student body (76 students) is served per day in the cafeteria. Three hundred ninety students are eligible for the free or price-reduced lunch, yet only 16 percent of these students take advantage of this free lunch. Numerous fast food restaurants and convenience stores with meals that are more appealing to the students than a nutritionally balanced school lunch surround East High School. Students complained that the food served in the cafeteria was not appetizing, and therefore, they justified paying more money for a lunch off campus. It was noted from the student focus groups that many students were not even aware of where the cafeteria was located. A food service operation in a public school is required by the United States Department of Agriculture to meet certain nutritional guidelines; therefore, the school menu has been designed to meet customer demands as well as the criteria for National School Lunch (NSL) Guidelines. If improvements are implemented, estimates indicate that participation levels could increase to 300 customers a day, representing 20 percent of the student body.

Stakeholders

Many stakeholder groups have supported this project. Foremost is the involvement and support of the administration, students, and faculty of East High School; the Director of the Department of Food and Nutrition Services; the central administration; and the manager and staff of the East High kitchen.

Target Markets

A number of different groups use the cafeteria including students, free and reduced-price customers, school clubs, and faculty. Currently, there are 648 students who qualify for the National School Lunch program, but only 3 percent participate.

There are more than 135 teachers and administrative staff at East High School daily, but only 12 to 20 use the cafeteria. This market segment is large and could be profitable, yet they are not being pursued. In the surveys and interviews with this segment, participants indicated that a majority of teachers bring their own lunch or buy from an area fast food restaurant and eat in the teacher's lounge on the third floor.

Dining Environment

Restaurants in the competitive marketplace not only focus on food quality, but also understand the significance of providing an attractive dining atmosphere. East High was fortunate that the dining hall that exists today provides adequate space to accommodate customers; however, the atmosphere was considered institutional. Redesigning the facility to be an attractive eating place would greatly increase its potential. Based on survey results, 75 percent of the student body said they would be more likely to eat in the cafeteria if attractive seating were provided. It was clear that the current seating plan was not conducive to creating a social environment.

Results

The first stage of this project was a competitive market analysis and student survey. They showed that students prefer a fast food or "food court" restaurant theme. Tables 1 and 2 clearly illustrate the results of the student survey.

National School Lunch program students had similar results to non eligible students. Thirty-two percent spent between $2.50 and $3.75 and 22 percent spent between $1.25 and $2.50. Students were also asked to rate the quality of food, cleanliness and service of the operation, and the decor. On a scale of 1 to 5 (5 being best), good food received a mean ranking of 3.5, cleanliness 3.0, price 2.5,

Table 1   Student Eating Habits

Where Students Eat	Regular Students (times per week)	National School Lunch (times per week)
Cafeteria	0.6	1.8
Bring lunch	1.3	1.0
Eat off campus	4.2	3.7

fast service 2.0, and decor 1.0. Students also indicated their food preferences. The following items were the most popular food preferences:

Most Popular Food

Pizza	Hamburgers	Sub sandwiches
Mexican food	Fresh fruit	Salad bar
Homemade cookies	Milk shakes	Coffee and tea

Food Service Operations

An analysis of both menu and environmental components of the food service operations revealed that with some redesign of the existing space and given the expected increase in customer participation levels, there would be a significant impact on several aspects of the food service operation. Five key operational issues need to be addressed in order to realize success in this pilot program: trash handling procedures, student monitoring, food production, cafeteria policies, and food storage.

Summary

The benefits associated with developing the cafeteria are unlimited. The cafeteria has had a negative perception for over a decade and changing the habits of the students will be difficult.

Table 2   Student Spending Habits

Grade level	<$1.25	$1.25–$2.50	$2.50–$3.75	$3.75–$4.75	$4.75–$6.75	>$6.75
Freshmen	5%	30%	40%	15%	5%	4%
Sophomores	7%	20%	48%	20%	1%	4%
Juniors	4%	20%	45%	22%	5%	4%
Seniors	3%	25%	33%	25%	10%	4%

Nonsubsidized students only. Some rows do not total to 100% due to rounding.

Questions

1. What changes might be recommended for the high school cafeteria that could be implemented given the constraints faced by a public school system?
2. Who should be involved in the decision-making process?
3. How will success be measured for any changes?

References

Denver Public Schools. Internal documents. 1995. Department of Food Services and Nutrition.

Richardson, M. E., R. Smith Erskine, and L. J. Boudreaux. 1990. School Food Service Supervisor's Involvement in Layout and Design of Facilities. *School Food Service Journal* 14 (2): 118–123.

Tsakalos, P., and M. Joynt. 1994. Not the Same Old Thing. *School Food Service Journal,* (February): 18–24.

The Employee Whose Personal Habits Defy Sanitation Guidelines

Objectives

At the completion of this case study, students should be able to:

1. Provide an example of an employee with a typical lack of comprehension, or a bad attitude, toward in-service training.
2. Prepare a manager for a situation with an unexpected outcome.
3. Explore ways to provide more meaningful sanitation instruction for employees.

Case Study Narrative

Julia, the manager of Bob's Barbeque and Ribs restaurant, entered the ladies room adjacent to the dining room. It was obvious from the conversation she overheard among the staff that were also using the ladies room that a production cook named Maria was in the stall next to her. After Julia finished using the lavatory, she washed her hands and was preparing to leave when Maria left the stall. She seemed to be in a hurry as she moved directly toward the exit door. It appeared that Maria was in such a hurry to get back to work that she had forgotten to wash her hands. Concerned about this lapse in Maria's hygiene, especially since there had been a recent in-service training session stressing cleanliness, Julia called out to Maria and asked, "Did you forget that according to protocol you should wash your hands before returning to work?" Maria replied, "I'm not going back to work, I'm going to lunch, so I can do what I want." With that said, Maria rushed from the room to get her lunch before a stunned Julia could think of a retort for what had just happened.

17

Questions

1. What should be Julia's immediate response to this situation?
2. What method should Julia use to discover why Maria has this attitude?
3. If this is an education or training issue, how should Julia change the training of cooks to make the sanitation issue more relevant to them?
4. What methods of follow-up training might be helpful in correcting Maria's outlook?

Marketing Ingenuity and Product Development

Objectives

At the completion of this case study, students should be able to:

1. Evaluate the niche market that the Denver Buffalo Company has developed.
2. Develop strategies to expand that niche or broaden market appeal for buffalo.
3. Examine the public policy issues associated with game meat production.
4. Evaluate the marketing strategies now in place for the Denver Buffalo Company.
5. Analyze the product development avenues available to the Denver Buffalo Company.

Case Study Narrative

Will McFarlane, president of the Denver Buffalo Company (DBC), said, "What we are doing with buffalo is as exciting and significant as what Steven Jobs did with Apple Computers." McFarlane and his partners at the DBC knew that to make any "real" money they would need to increase their yield and profit. Their problem was to create and market value-added products that would increase the yield from the buffalo and still sell prime cuts. He realized that product development and marketing in the agricultural industry had many hurdles.

The Challenge

The creation of value-added buffalo meat products to improve the yield of servable meat and therefore increase profits is the objective of the DBC. This objective has proven to be a challenging one for the DBC partners. DBC Marketing, the

19

parent company of DBC, has created and is developing a niche for buffalo (bison) meat. Niche marketing is becoming a way of life in most industries and the meat industry is no different. The ideal niche, according to Kotler (1980), has sufficient size and purchasing power to be profitable, has growth potential, and has been bypassed or neglected by major competitors. The firm in the ideal niche has superior competencies to serve the niche effectively and can defend its position against an attack by major competitors because of existing good will. Perhaps a key to the ideal niche is exemplified in the ABCD Rule of successful niche marketing, "Always Be Collecting Data" (Linneman and Stanton 1991). To be successful, a niche marketer needs to have a strategy for creating value.

The Denver Buffalo Company

The Denver Buffalo Company, a subsidiary of DBC Marketing located in Denver, Colorado, is the only buffalo marketing company that buys, raises, feeds, slaughters, and then develops and sells buffalo products. The company holdings include the 14,000-acre Sweet Ranch located near Kiowa, Colorado, which includes a breeding herd of more than 1,200 buffalo and a feed lot holding approximately 800 buffalo, as well as a restaurant/deli/art gallery, also called the Denver Buffalo Company, located near downtown Denver.

The DBC is operated with a small number of employees that include the founder; three vice presidents of operations, marketing, and sales; plus a small sales staff, office personnel, a ranch foreman and several ranch hands, a meat processing expert who represents DBC at various co-packers; and the managers and employees of the DBC restaurant.

Buffalo Sales Strategies

As a leader in a niche market, the DBC must educate consumers about buffalo as well as market buffalo products. On average, buffalo costs 50 to 75 percent more than cattle. Conversely, a buffalo is expected to generate twice the revenue of beef cattle. Expectations are that a one thousand pound, $1,300 buffalo can generate $2,500 in revenue from meat and an undetermined amount for other products such as skulls ($200 each), hides, rugs ($400 each), stuffed heads ($2,500 each), and buffalo coats ($1,650 each), plus additional revenues for currently unused by products such as bones and organ meat.

To sell buffalo meat products, DBC's marketing strategy stresses the healthiness and naturalness of buffalo. The company is able to back up its claims by citing a variety of research conducted by the United States Department of Agriculture, the University of North Dakota, and other institutions. DBC's key selling points are that buffalo is an all-natural meat grown without the use of hormones or any growth stimulants. It is high in protein, low in fat, cholesterol, and calories; nonallergenic; high in B-vitamins and iron; high in linolenic, palmitic, and stearic acids; and is a highly nutrient dense food.

There is an economic issue. A 100 percent natural buffalo product commands a premium price. Buffalo is a more expensive product than beef; therefore, buffalo hot dogs and other products that must compete with beef cattle products are at a pricing disadvantage, except perhaps in gourmet food stores. Of the actual useable product, approximately 20 percent consists of prime cuts. Eighty percent of the usable meat is used in value-added products such as hot dogs and jerky. The DBC partners recognized early that grinding buffalo into burger has traditionally been the simplest solution to using buffalo meat not cut for steaks and ribs, but they also realized that this was not a very profitable alternative.

To take advantage of both their healthy image and the cost conscious mass market, the DBC partners decided to develop two lines of buffalo products. The original lines of products on the DBC label are 100 percent buffalo. In order to compete with beef products on a wider scale and appeal to a mass market, the DBC developed "Buffalo Will's" line of products in which between 40 and 49 percent natural beef has been added to buffalo meat products. This accomplishes several things. It allows the development of an additional line of products as well as making buffalo products more price acceptable to the consumer, and it allows the use of sodium nitrite (prohibited in buffalo) in the Buffalo Will's products. Products under each brand name are:

Denver Buffalo Company Label

Fajita meat; Ground buffalo; Buffalo patties; Roasts; Stew meat; Jerky, pepperoni, teriyaki, original, spicy Cajun; Back ribs; Brisket; Flank steak; Rounds; Rib-eyes; Liver; Tenderloin; Short ribs; Strip loin; Tongue; Tri-tip; Trim; Top round.

Buffalo Will's Label

Bologna, Bratwurst, Salami, Franks, Polish sausage, Italian sausage, Pizza Crumbles, Summer sausage.

Government Regulation Implications

One of the DBC's key concerns must be that buffalo is considered by the United States Department of Agriculture (USDA) to be a wild game animal similar to venison or elk. Federal regulations prohibit the interstate sale of beef, pork, lamb, veal, or equine meats without a federal inspection. However, federal inspection of buffalo is voluntary; buffalo can be shipped across state lines with state inspection. From a marketing standpoint, the DBC officials feel that customer perception will be improved if buffalo meat is federally inspected. The cost of federal inspection is $30 to $35 per hour. These costs are above the costs for inspection of beef, lamb, pork and such, presenting the buffalo industry with a competitive disadvantage.

In addition, to ship value-added buffalo products across state lines, the DBC would like to use sodium nitrite, a preservative in meat products. The Food and Drug Administration (FDA), part of the USDA, which oversees shipping meat across state lines, restricts the use of sodium nitrite products because it has been linked to cancer in some studies. Beef products are allowed to use sodium nitrite because the FDA exempted them from the sodium nitrite regulations with a grandfather clause. Only by including more than 3 percent of an amenable meat (i.e., beef cattle) with the buffalo meat, can wild game products be permitted to use sodium nitrite.

The DBC partners feel that using sodium nitrite would assist in preserving the buffalo product during shipping. They are wary, however, because this process requires the DBC package labels to inform the consumer that beef has been added to the buffalo (no maximum percentage is specified). The final DBC product remains all natural because Coleman's All Natural Beef is used; however, the DBC partners fear that not being able to represent their product as 100 percent buffalo might endanger their all natural and healthy image. The partners and industry trade association representatives are lobbying government officials to explore changing existing regulations.

Target Markets

Marketing officials for the DBC identified retail supermarkets, restaurants and other commercial food service operations, specialty food stores, convenience stores, and specialty retail locations as their target markets.

Supply of Product

Cattle ranchers do not perceive the buffalo business as a major threat to the beef cattle business. There are only a handful of ranches in North America that have buffalo herds of more than 1,000 head. For example, in addition to the Sweet Ranch herd, Ted Turner, the cable television mogul, has converted his Montana and New Mexico ranches from cattle to buffalo and has approximately 5,000 head. There are other large ranches raising buffalo throughout the west.

Competition at All Levels of the Market

The DBC faces competition at all levels of its marketing channel. In the distribution segment of the buffalo business, several Denver area companies (Dale's Exotic Meats, Rocky Mountain Game, and Rocky Mountain Natural Meats) market and distribute buffalo meat products. Restaurant competition for the DBC own restaurant includes Denver area signature restaurants such as The Fort in Morrison, Colorado, the Buckhorn Exchange in Denver, the Buffalo Restaurant and Bar in Idaho Springs, and the Mountain Man Steak House and Saloon in Commerce City. Ranching competition exists, as noted earlier, but it is limited in size and scope. The real competition that the DBC faces is on a product-to-product level in supermarkets. While not a major threat to beef, the competition for shelf space in the supermarkets and for menu items is great. This competition goes beyond beef to include pork, poultry, lamb, and other specialty meats in the market such as musk ox, elk, moose, ostrich, and alligator.

Promotion

The DBC has a small marketing and sales staff that works with brokers and distributors to sell its products. They have used a variety of strategies to market buffalo products including advertising, competitive pricing, developing a reputation for consistency in quantity and quality, USDA inspection, nutritional value, and customer service. The DBC partners feel that a key part of the DBC effort is the education of the food brokers and distributors about buffalo. To sell the product requires knowledge of the taste, cooking methods, yield, prices, and uses of buffalo that will best fit the markets being targeted.

What's Next?

The task of the DBC is to make the buffalo niche big enough for the business to be truly profitable. McFarlane said, "Rather than be just part of the big herd, you want to be right there focused on the niche." If we want to bring back the great herds, if we want the number of buffalo to climb back into the millions, we have to make buffalo commercially viable. How to do all this and still make money is something the DBC partners continually ask themselves. They wonder whether this will be a fine business or an expensive hobby.

Questions

1. Identify the target markets that would best serve the needs of the Denver Buffalo Company. Has the Denver Buffalo Company been right so far? Are there new markets to explore, or do they have enough going on right now?
2. Formulate marketing strategies that could be used to reach these markets and develop promotional strategies for specific product lines.
3. Develop a strategy to enact governmental change concerning laws for shipping and inspecting buffalo.
4. Are beef cattle ranchers really going to ignore the buffalo industry?
5. Are there new markets that might be receptive to buffalo products (for example, Japan, Korea, Europe, Australia)? What are the potential problems of developing such markets?

References

Denver Buffalo Company. 1993. Promotional materials. Denver: Denver Buffalo Company.

Hutchinson, J. 1993. Riding Herd on the Red Meat of the 90's. *Colorado Business Magazine* (February): 14.

Kotler, P. 1980. *Marketing management: Analysis, planning and control,* Englewood Cliffs: Prentice Hall.

Linneman, R.E., and J. L. Stanton, 1991. *Making Niche Marketing Work.* New York: McGraw Hill.

Vending Opportunities

Objectives

At the completion of the case study, students should be able to:

1. Explain the vending sector and its profile as a business.
2. Evaluate a site for vending products.
3. List the options available in the vending product market.

Case Study Narrative

A campus food service manager has been charged with creating new lines of revenue. Through preliminary research, he has identified vending as a potential new segment. Vending is a growing sector of the food service and contract management businesses approaching 30 billion dollars annually (NAMA 2001). Generally considered an unattended point of sale, vending can provide food service supplies and a variety of products to consumers at diverse venues. Traditionally, vending has meant coffee service for an office and soda pop, candy, and cigarettes. Today vending has evolved to provide a full line of products and services, including hot or refrigerated foods, dairy products, french fries, sandwiches, popcorn, and so on. To no one's surprise, canned soda dominates the vending markets in this country; there are Coca Cola or Pepsi machines in practically every building in America. Vending serves a diverse line of businesses including hospitals, schools, colleges, office buildings, manufacturing plants, arenas, stadiums, natural recreation areas, apartment complexes, fitness centers, car dealerships, and more.

At a large Midwestern university, the vending and food service contracts had traditionally been separate, but an opportunity had arisen to provide a vending contract along with the food service contract. The issue for the food service management company that held the food service contract at the university was that the manager and the staff lacked experience with vending and, therefore, there was a reluctance to take on a risky venture. The general manager of food service was interested in pursuing the vending contract, and his research indicated a number of issues that he needed to control in order to make a strong proposal. These included the market, service, demand, finance, and security issues in support of his proposal.

Market

Vending, like any other business, must market itself to consumers and potential clients. To evaluate campus vending points of service, the four Ps (product, price, place, and promotion) need to be considered. The key target market for the campus is students. They are primarily interested in quick, low-cost, satisfying products and their needs include availability at nontraditional times of day. Additional markets are faculty, staff, and visitors to the campus. The management company needs to know what portion of these segments would use vending machines and what types of machines and products are preferred.

Service

Equipment is a key factor in vending considerations. Maintenance, service, and repair of vending equipment are critical in a vending contract. The personnel needed to service the equipment and maintain the day-to-day relationship with a client are also critical in terms of reliability, efficiency, and expertise. Industry experts suggest allocating 20 minutes per machine plus travel time for regular checks of vending equipment.

Demand

Demand for vending services must be assessed for the market and financially to properly evaluate the marketability and feasibility of a vending operation. An area review of the university identified some of the following issues, questions, and facts.

The food service manager started with a profile of the campus and proceeded to develop a plan of action to propose a vending contract bid. The university officials were looking for something new in vending and wanted the most up-to-date offerings in unique locations. Students, in their feedback to university officials, often complained about the lack of food service and vending in the evening and in study locations across the campus. University data from an informal poll indicated that more than 10 percent of the student body would use vending locations if the products were maintained and upgraded from current standards. Other data collected include the following:

- The university is an accredited institution.
- Brand names are being used.
- The main campus is located in an urban area.
- The campus encompasses over 1,200 acres on six sites.
- Total enrollment is 22,000, 14,000 undergraduate and 8,000 graduate, with 65 percent commuters and 35 percent residential.
- The vending equipment being used is older; newer technologies are available.
- Selling prices are consistent with the market; for example, $1.50 for a canned soda.
- Access to water and electric is adequate.
- The current vendor is not sharing information about existing sales of canned soda, cigarettes, and candy.
- Electronically up-to-date information repositories in the region are available in the library.
- State-of-the-art computing facilities for student and faculty use are scattered across campus.

In addition to all the previous factors, vending, like a hotel or a restaurant, is heavily influenced by "location, location, and location." Facility layout and design are contingent on traffic flow, access, and visibility. The campus food service manager suggested dormitories, classroom buildings with a large proportion of night classes scheduled, and more remote areas of the campus as possible vending sites.

The account manager has targeted twenty-two academic and administrative buildings as potential vending sites, as well as eight residence halls. The issue for the account manager will be placement, product, and potential demand. The vending product mix has changed from the original four Cs (coffee, canned soda, candy, and cigarettes). Today's choices include a variety of snacks, bottled water, flavored coffees, juices, larger sizes of products, and dietary products. Business practices for vending operations are not unique, but they differ slightly from the practices of some other businesses. Inventory is obviously critical, as are machine service, route management for the truck delivery systems, route recordkeeping, cash management for the machines, and product requisition.

In addition to internal information, a review of competitors in the area is also needed. This would include identifying other vending outlets, convenience stores, and quick-service restaurants. Vending, to be competitive, must offer good products, good selection, service, good prices, and attractive packaging. The local competition consists of quick-service restaurants five minutes away, located on a major east/west road, including Taco Bell, MacDonald's, Subway, a local Mexican quick-service restaurant, and a deli. The food service management company also has three food courts and dormitory feeding areas in the residence halls on the campus. Consumers have been trained by society to eat away from home, eat quickly, and expect to have a choice in their selections. The vending business is positioned well to take advantage of these market factors.

Finance

The financial aspects of vending must also be explored. In addition to the prices, the current commissions, initial investment and potential sales, and cost must be forecast. Industry experts suggest examination of three concepts:

- Return on sales
- Payback
- Return on investment (NAMA 2002)

A typical operating statement for a vending operation includes sales, product costs, labor costs, commissions, and miscellaneous operating costs in order to determine operating profit. Volume can often make the difference between profit and loss. Critical mass, or sufficient market demand, is a key factor for the vendor operator.

A sample profit and loss statement might resemble the following (NAMA 2002):

Sales	100.0%
Product Cost	45.7
Gross Margin	54.3
Labor Costs	22.1
Commissions	9.3
Other Costs	18.6
Operating Profit	4.3%

The vending industry also provides some simple statistics to guide potential vending operators. Different vending combinations of product and machines can yield from $1,125 per month to $4,500 per month (Vending Statistics).

There are start-up costs, and more than two-thirds of vending businesses own their own machines. Regular financing is available, and new ventures can be directed through association membership to machine manufacturers, banks, commercial finance companies, and equipment leasing companies.

Security

Security and lighting needs are critical for vending to ensure the continued maintenance of the machinery and to prevent vandalism. It is important to remember that the majority of vending is a cash business. Therefore, security is important. Operationally, for the vending operator, this emphasizes the importance of cash management.

Summary

The vending industry has been assisted through improved technology and machinery, inventory controls and rotation, and timely service. The industry, however, does have its detractors and potential problems. Hygiene, food safety, and additional equipment needs (such as microwaves, change machines, and debit card systems) all increase the complexity of the vending business. It is still an underdeveloped market and is arguably the easiest branding investment a business can make. Vending is here to stay and provides consumers with an excellent source of trial purchases.

Vending business start-ups and vending placement decisions, made in a business-like manner, can yield positive and sustainable results. There are many factors for the food service management company to consider. A successful new venture could make the food service manager the leader in his or her company in vending and help his or her career. A mistake due to lack of data and research could be costly. The account manager, in the university situation described above, sought input from a variety of sources and asked a class on the campus to investigate vending machines and products and make some recommendations. The professor for the course saw this as an opportunity for his students to deal with a real life situation.

Questions

1. What additional data should the food service company collect in preparing to respond to a request for proposal?
2. What are the unique technologies that might be available for implementation on the campus?
3. What are the hurdles for operating such a large account?
4. What are the labor issues involved in this venture?
5. Is the estimated 10 percent of the market that would use the vending machines a big enough piece of business to make the vending worthwhile? How could that percentage be increased?

References

NAMA. 2001. http://www.vending.org/about_vending/vending101.html. Vending 101.

Student Information about the Vending Industry. 2001. http://www.avab.org .uk/avab/students.html, pp. 1–7.

Vendors North Carolina. 2001. Wysiwyg://28/http://vendorsnc.ecorp.net/faq.htm. Frequently Asked Questions, pp. 1–6.

Vending Statistics. 2002. http://www.123vending.com/venmacstatof.html

The Buses Are Coming!

A Management Planning Case Study

Objectives

At the completion of the case study, students should be able to:

1. Learn to examine the interdependency of food service system components when developing management plans.
2. Develop comprehensive, multidimensional management plans that take into account food service system component interdependencies.
3. Think "outside the box" to effectively take advantage of sales opportunities.

Case Study Narrative

Background Information

Buffets, Inc., founded in 1983, is now the nation's thirteenth largest restaurant chain. Their buffet restaurants use a "scatter" buffet system that allows for a wide selection of food and easier access than traditional buffets. The company's focus is traditional "home cooking" served in a friendly, family-oriented environment. It strives to set the quality of the food apart from other restaurants in the buffet category. This is achieved using fresh, high-quality ingredients and by preparing food items in small quantities (enough to feed 8 to 12 guests) at continual intervals throughout the day. The meals include beverage and dessert for one low price. The restaurants serve lunch and dinner daily, and most of the restaurants offer weekend breakfast.

The Harrisburg, Pennsylvania, Old Country Buffet restaurant opened in January 1996. The restaurant is located in a strip mall on Jonestown Road in a

30

busy commercial district. An entry/exit from Route 81, which runs from New York through Pennsylvania and down to southern states, is less than two miles from the restaurant. The strip mall has a Media Play, a SuperPetz, and a Hills discount department store. A pylon sign erected on Jonestown Road and travel signs on Route 81 increase visibility. There is sufficient parking available in the strip mall for cars and buses, and bus parking is available behind the restaurant as well. The restaurant is entirely nonsmoking; it is open from 10:30 A.M. until 9:00 P.M. weekdays and 8:00 A.M. until 10:00 P.M. on weekends. Lunch guests are typically retirees, businesspeople, and some families with nonschool-age children. Dinner guests are primarily families and couples.

The restaurant seats 386 people in a variety of four-person booths; moveable two, four, and six top tables; and a banquet room attached to the main dining room. There is one restaurant entry door that accesses a long queue, at the end of which are two POS (point-of-service) registers. Typically only one register is used, but the second is opened during high-volume times when many seats are available. Cashiers work quickly so even during high-volume times the second register is opened only as needed to keep the dining area full. There is one exit door, but there are several emergency exits. During high-volume times, greeters meet guests after they have paid and direct guests to open tables. Wireless communicators are often used because of the rapid pace of seating and the large size of the dining area. The main greeter directs the guests to a secondary greeter who waits by the available table and informs first-time guests about the buffet process.

When they are ready, guests head toward the "scatter" buffet tables. There are two separate salad bars. One offers make-it-yourself salads and fresh cut fruit; the other features prepared salads such as coleslaw, potato salad, pasta salad, spinach salad, and other salads offered on a cyclical basis. This buffet table also offers two soups daily. There are three hot-food buffet bars. The front buffet bar offers a variety of entrées and side items. These items rotate according to the cyclical menu. The second hot-food bar offers staple entrée items such as fried and baked chicken, fried and baked fish, and french fries. This bar also has a double carving station. During lunch service this carving station is used to run out leftovers or offer additional menu items, while at dinner a carver offers at least two hand-carved meats there. The third hot bar offers staple side items such as mashed potatoes and gravy and vegetables such as green beans, corn, and carrots. There are some cyclical items on this bar as specified by the menu. There are two other buffet tables. One offers drinks such as soda, iced tea, milk, and coffee. The final table offers an extensive variety of desserts, including hot cobblers, cinnamon rolls and muffins, cakes, cookies, and ice cream. Several employees, called line attendants, are necessary to maintain the food and cleanliness of these buffet tables. Since the restaurant's focus is on home cooking using high-quality food prepared in small fresh batches, many guests come back for second helpings. Dining room attendants work in the dining area to clear tables, keep the area clean, offer guest assistance, and make the guests feel welcome.

The kitchen is a suitable size for a high-volume, conventional food production operation. There is a cold prep area with a walk-in cooler. Prepared and do-it-yourself salads are prepared in this area. The cook's line features standard equipment, such as fryers, griddles, conventional and convection ovens, steam kettles, steamers, a large bain marie for soups and sauces, and four hot holding cabinets. There is some worktable space, but the area is hard to use for prep during peak times. A maximum of five cooks can work the line; otherwise it becomes too crowded. The cooks have easy access to a walk-in cooler and freezer, dry storage, and a walk-in chicken cooler. The dish room is right next to the cook's line, and there is a pass-through window to send dirty pans to the pot sink. The dish room has a three-bay pot sink and a very large flight-type dishwasher. There is an exit to the rear of the operation from the dish area. Product orders are received and trash is removed through this door. There is an access hallway from the dish room to the dining area so that dining room attendants can bring back bus carts with the dirty dishes. There is a separate chicken breading area. All of the fried and baked chicken comes in fresh and is prepared or breaded on-site. Both are high-demand items. Elderly guests often prefer the baked chicken, while younger guests eat more of the fried foods. The last area in the kitchen is the bakery. This area is on the opposite side of the dish room from the cook's line and the walk-in coolers and freezers. The bakery supplies the dessert bar and dinner rolls to the hot food bars. Line attendants use the entry to this bakery area to transport empty pans from the buffet tables to the dish area.

The restaurant has five managers and around seventy to eighty employees on staff. The managers have been with the operation since opening day and usually work five days per week. Typical management scheduling is three managers per day. The remaining management shifts are scheduled depending on needs and sales projections. Typically, around 1,800 employee hours are scheduled per week. Those hours are 55 percent FOH (front-of-house) and 45 percent BOH (back-of-house). FOH positions are cashier, greeter, dining room attendant, and line attendant. BOH positions are line cook, cold prep, baker, dish area, chicken breader, and maintenance. Many employees are cross-trained and are used to being shifted in positions, although dining room attendants tend to like to stay in that position.

The Situation

It is one week before Good Friday. The general manager, Bob Jackson, just received a call from a tour bus operator that twelve buses carrying thirty to forty high school students each will be arriving, at the same time, at his operation sometime between 12:30 P.M. and 1:45 P.M. on Good Friday. Each person will pay for himself or herself.

Bob normally serves between 500 and 600 meals on Fridays between the hours of 10:30 A.M. and 3:30 P.M. About 150 people arrive between 2:30 P.M. and

3:30 P.M. to beat the dinner price increase at 3:30 P.M. Normal scheduling for a Friday lunch is four table servers/bus people, one cashier, five buffet servers, four cooks, one cold prep, one baker, and three dishwashers. The opening and the mid-shift managers work lunch service. Foods on the buffet include the make-it-yourself and prepared salad bar with soups, the beverage bar, the dessert bar, and the three hot food bars. The carver station hot bar has four hotel-pan-size steam units that offer fried and baked chicken, fried and baked fish, french fries, and baked potatoes with broccoli and cheese sauce in separate pans, and there are two half-hotel pan slots for leftovers. The fries, fried fish, and broccoli and cheese sauce are in quarter hotel pans and the rest are in half-hotel pans. The front hot buffet bar has five hotel-pan-size steam units, a full hotel pan of dinner rolls, and half-hotel pans of macaroni and cheese, seafood patties, a sautéed vegetable, beef patties, red potatoes, baked beans, pizza, and chicken with dumplings. The other hot bar has four hotel-pan-size units, and half-hotel pans of fruit muffins, mashed potatoes, gravy, carrots, green beans, cut corn, seafood quiche, and corn muffins. All silverware, plates, and glasses are kept available at the food bars.

Questions

Assume you are Bob Jackson, the general manager of this operation.

1. Examine the guest count projections and compare it to the normal Friday lunch employee and management schedule.
   a. Do you have enough labor scheduled to properly serve the number of guests?
   b. How would you alter the schedule to ensure that you can offer proper service? (Be specific as to how many employees you would add per position and explain your reasoning.)
   c. Is there anything else that you should do with respect to the employees to make sure that the reservation is successful for the operation?
2. Examine the likely food preferences of the different customer groups that the operation would serve for lunch.
   a. What types of foods offered by Buffets, Inc., would the typical lunch guest prefer? (Be specific.)
   b. What type of foods offered by Buffets, Inc., would the reservation guests prefer? (Be specific.)
   c. Are there any changes you would make to the food being offered and, if so, what and how would you do it? (Be specific.)
3. The reservation guests are going to pay individually as they come in. Is this good or would it be better for them to prepay? Explain your answer taking into account the impact the payment method could have on guest flow and FOH and BOH operation.

Rebidding the Contract

Objectives

At the completion of the case study, students should be able to:

1. Recognize and list key components of the bidding process.
2. Evaluate and explain the advantages or disadvantages of each company.
3. Identify what the issues for consideration are when reviewing a bid.

Case Study Narrative

Introduction

The Director of Student Services at a medium-sized university, Tom Bannock, reviewed the operations of the food service on campus. The contract with the current food service management company would expire soon. Discussions among the university administrators concerning the food service management company focused on performance and satisfaction. Bannock was new to the campus and was not familiar with the company except through student comments and an occasional meal at the student center. Bannock was the liaison with the food service management company. He did not have the final decision-making authority concerning the contract but was asked to make a recommendation concerning the possibility of sending the contract out for bid. He considered his facts and the input he had received from colleagues and wondered if the university could do better. He recommended that the contract be opened for bid. The central administrators of the university agreed, and the bidding process began.

The Incumbent

The company that currently holds the contract for campus food service has been the food service provider for thirteen years. The account is complex. The food service that needs to be provided includes dining-hall board plans and retail dining on two campuses, catering on and off campus for university-related events and banquets, and concession operations at the university's hockey and basketball arena. Annual revenues for the account were approximately $9 million. The present general manager is experienced at this account and was promoted from a department director to general manager in the last year.*

The day-to-day liaison for the university with the food service company had always been the Director of Student Services. Previously the rapport with this office had been outstanding. The general manager and the other food service management company officials always have had an open exchange of ideas and information, which made the relationship beneficial. However, the new Director does not share this history with the company and could only use the information he has had available to him for the six months he has been at the university.

The president of the food service management company is a distinguished alumnus from the university, who majored in hotel and restaurant management. He has always been proud of his university, and retaining this account would be a source of pride for him and a consideration for the fundraising office of the university.

Food service management company officials feel they have always had a good relationship with the campus community, including students, faculty, and staff. The company has always hired students for work during the school year, as well as hiring students for permanent positions and placement around the country.

The district manager for the food service company, Alan Black, knew that rebidding the account was always a possibility, but admitted to some surprise when he was informed that the contract would go out for bid. He was not sure of the reasons for the decision, but understood the realities of the situation. In a letter to the university administration he wrote, "Any contractual association can and must be reviewed." The incumbent, while admitting to a feeling of tension and anxiety, "welcomed the competition." After all, the food service company was a national leader in contract food service and campus dining and could compete with anyone. Black and company officials felt that the rebidding process would allow them to conduct a self-assessment of their performance and assess their relationship with the university.

---

*This case was originally written as a result of a CHRIE Faculty Internship and is used with the permission of International CHRIE.

The University

The university has a total population of 8,000 students, a small portion of whom live in four residence halls. Much of the student body commutes to the campus and would potentially use the retail dining facilities. The general goals of the university are a quality food service program using a company that can maintain a good working relationship with the university community.

The thirteen-year association between the university and the current food service contractor also included capital investments by the contractor to improve the dining facilities on the campus. The successful food service management company bid would have to include a commitment for additional funds for capital investment in campus food service facilities.

The university's fundraising officials have no standing in the rebid decision officially, but they want to have input before any final decision is made. Thus, the rebidding process took on a political slant, at least for some members of the university.

The Food Service Committee

As the rebidding process began in earnest, a team of people was selected by the university administrators to evaluate proposals from companies bidding on the food service contract. This team included Tom Bannock as Director of Student Services, a vice president of finance, a faculty member, several students representing all facets of the student body, a chef employee of the university (not part of the contractor team), residence hall directors, and the student center director. Each member of the committee was part of the campus community. Through their familiarity with the campus, all had ideas that they believed would best serve the university. For example, some members of the team promoted the idea of more franchise brands on the campus sold from mobile carts similar to those at stadiums and arenas. This type of suggestion and others were made to each company bidding on the food service account.

Few of the committee members had any experience in or any practical knowledge of food service as a business. Thus, each committee member had to be educated on how food service is managed, hopefully gaining some understanding from the perspective of the bidding company. In addition, the university hired a food service consultant to conduct an operational review of the food service operation on the campuses and make recommendations to them about what should be done with the food service. The committee planned to use the report written by the consultant as a guideline document for evaluating proposals.

Food service committee evaluation procedures included reviewing the written proposals as well as visiting other campuses managed by the bidding companies. Each company gave a formal sales presentation to the committee and held meetings with the committee that included sales managers, district managers, and vice presidents of each company. The committee was charged with making a recommendation to the president for a food service contractor. Therefore, committee members were responsible for making a decision that potentially could impact the campus for years to come.

Competitors

The account was offered for bid, and requests for proposals (RFPs) were sent out to a number of food service contractors. Initially, five companies indicated they would bid for the account, though one of these withdrew early in the process. The four remaining companies were nationally known and had good reputations in the contract food service field in general and campus dining in particular. Each company crafted its proposal based on the requirements of the RFP, committee input, student opinion, and its own expertise and ideas for the account.

The Proposals

Each company submitted a multivolume proposal to the university food service committee for consideration. Components of the proposals generally followed these outlines:

Company 1
(Incumbent)
Executive summary
Qualifications
Plan of operations for each venue
Management systems
Financial proposals
Menu cycles
Marketing

Company 3
Executive summary
Operational plans

Qualifications
Menu pricing
Conferences
Improvements
Responsibilities

Company 2
Executive summary
Operational plans
Summer programs
Menus
Marketing programs
Organization and operation
Staffing
Transition
Qualifications
Improvements
Terms and conditions

Company 4
Executive summary
Operational review
Marketing
Recommended menu
Organization and operation
Policies

Company 4 (*contd.*)
Staffing
Transition
Standards
Qualifications
Menu pricing
Improvements
Responsibilities
Terms and conditions

Each food service company also included information on its willingness to invest in the future of the campus, which would create a long-term relationship with the university. Capital improvements and the company's ability to invest in the campus financially were key proposal components. Specific amounts of money to be committed to the capital improvement projects on the campus were also included. In addition, the usual buy-back procedures for these funds were outlined. The incumbent was not offering the largest amount of money in this process and feared that a competitor would attempt to buy the account. The university had slated the student center for renovation, and the food service company would be a big part of that process. However, there was no concrete information on what the university wanted to do or whether there was a market for any suggested changes.

Financial information on the cost to the students, the savings to the university, and the profit expectations for each company was also explained in each proposal. Each company also conducted student surveys to collect decision-making data and stress that they were market driven as well as sensitive to the needs of the client.

Student Input

All students were encouraged to participate in the food service survey process, including dormitory residents who would have a board plan, commuting students who would only eat in retail areas, and fraternity and sorority members who had their own food service programs in their houses and, therefore, were mainly interested in the retail areas. Student opinion was a key factor in designing a proposal that would be successful. The university had based some of the decision to rebid the contract on the premise that there was a level of dissatisfaction with the current service being provided. The current inflexibility of the meal plans and services being offered was a key factor in developing the service proposals for all competing companies. The students wanted flexibility in the food service program and a more interactive approach for food service. This translated into self-service buffets, demonstration cooking, national brands, and flexible hours.

Student input from the surveys focused on such things as take-out food, access to national brands, convenience stores, all-day service, and upscale products. Food concepts and specific requests varied from salads, fresh fruit, and Italian foods to health foods and pizza.

Students generally felt that the prices of the food plans and the pricing in the retail areas were fair. While some students expressed dissatisfaction, the pricing structure was competitive with local restaurant and food service alternatives.

Was there enough dissatisfaction to change food service contractors? Students, while participating in the survey, did not attend the company presentations, nor did they review the proposals made available to them in any large number.

Client Input on Management

Student input was important to the process, but each company also understood that the university was the client, and equally important to student satisfaction were financial considerations and the ability of the company to work with the university.

The incumbent's relationship with the university contacts had generally been good, especially at the district manager level, although Alan Beck had detected some conflict between the existing general manager and Tom Bannock. It was vital to the university that the relationship with the food service contractor and their on-campus representatives be a good one. The university wanted someone who would work with them, as well as interact with students and faculty on the campus.

The incumbent, who had other accounts nearby, considered that it could easily swap managers from one account to another. The competitors, who also had a presence in the same geographic area, felt that the issue of the unit general manager did not play a major part in the bid and proposal process. The burden of the proposal process fell primarily on district and national sales managers.

Conclusion

The bid processes for the university food service account began in February, and recommendations from the committee were to be delivered to the president's office by graduation in early June. The deadline was pushed back to the last week of June. The delays in the final decision and announcement of whom the account had been awarded to indicated that the decision was a difficult one and that the incumbent company might potentially lose the account. These delays also spurred a flurry of last-minute activity by company representatives involving meetings and telephone calls. Lobbying focused on the president of the university.

The university was concerned with getting the best deal for itself and its students. The incumbent company was hoping that familiarity had not bred contempt and that it would be given an equal opportunity to compete. It even offered to replace the general manager. The other three competing companies all hoped the university would honestly consider their proposals and not give unfair advantage to the incumbent company.

The decision to rebid the contract was not spurred by any glaring defect in the service or breach of contract. The university's motives were for the best deal possible and a quality food service program for the university. The incumbent still felt that it did not know what the client wanted. If looking for the best deal and a quality program were the real issues, would a different company be able to satisfy the client? A decision had to be made to award the account to one of the four companies. The final decision would be made by the university president.

Questions

1. How would you improve the bidding process from the university's or the company's position?
2. What were the intangible advantages or disadvantages that one company had over another?
3. Who should make the decision on the food service contract, and what are the key factors in this process?

Cases in Lodging Management

Leadership Expectations at the Benson Hotel

Objectives

At the completion of the case study, students should be able to:

1. Contrast and prioritize conflicting human resource and operational issues in a mid-sized independent operation.
2. Define leadership characteristics and values required to "turnaround" the Benson Hotel.
3. Identify and clarify supervisory responsibility.

Case Study Narrative

The Benson Hotel, a mid-sized independent property required new leadership. Mike Schwartz, Vice-president of Operations, pondered his next move as he reviewed last month's financial statements. The Benson was an eighty-five-room three-star property with a full-service restaurant, lounge, and banquet and health club facilities. The rapidly changing marketplace and new competition from well-established franchises had made Mike's job and the Benson's position more tenuous. Mike decided to commission a consultant's report on the property. He called up his longtime friend Jim Burke, who had worked for major chains across the country and was now a hospitality consultant.

"Jim, how are you old buddy?" Mike asked.

"I'm doing very well Mike. This consulting work has run me off my feet. What can I do for you?" Jim asked.

"Well Jim, I need an independent review of the Benson. We're holding our own but these franchise guys with their management contracts are really getting aggressive," Mike said.

43

"Yes, I know what you mean Mike. I have just completed a marketing study for a new building across town. These guys have some great programs. You have to try and stay ahead of them," said Jim.

Mike asked, "Do you think you could visit the property and have some lunch next week? I would like to start with an employee survey and some site work. You'll be working alongside my general manager, Sean Waters. Sean's been with us for about two years. Jim, I have some concerns about this guy and I'd like to have a fresh set of eyes look at what's going on at the Benson. Okay?"

Jim hesitated, "Okay Mike. How about next Thursday 10:00 a.m.? I'll meet you in the lobby."

"Wonderful, Jim. We'll see you then."

Sean Waters had been recruited by Mike as a rising star. Sean's background led Mike to believe he possessed a true spirit for hospitality, especially in the food service area. Sean had worked his way up in reputable full-service properties and restaurants while completing an undergraduate degree in hospitality. So, what had gone so wrong at the Benson for Mike to feel he needed to bring in a consultant to figure it out? Three months later Mike had an interim report on his desk.

Physical Plant Priorities

The following is a review of specific areas of the Benson Hotel that require attention.

Sales Office.   Located just off the lobby, this space is open to the public and is well below standards for this level of property. The property has worked hard to attract the corporate market. A well-renovated business center shared with a working sales area would enhance this area greatly.

Banquet Servery.   Located on the lower level from the main kitchen, this area seems more of a storage area, in fact this could serve as a limited holding area for banquet service. There is no counterspace and no secure shelving to store dishes, glassware, or cutlery. Floors and walls are in need of refinishing. Guests have gained access to this area on occasion.

Exterior Garbage Area.   The main compactor located in the rear parking lot of the hotel should be enclosed. It is unsightly to guests and can be viewed from the road by surrounding residences. A possible solution would be to pour a concrete slab allowing for drainage and build an enclosure on three sides to ensure access for pick-up.

Access for Persons with Disabilities.   Presently, the Benson has no access or rooms for guests with disabilities. At least two units should be converted for this purpose. The main reconfigurations are the bathrooms and doorways. On a few occasions guests with disabilities were observed leaving the hotel for other properties in the area that had such facilities. It is a good marketing initiative and may become necessary to maintain the rating of the property.

Lobby. The lobby chairs and broadloom should be upgraded to reflect the marketplace and reputation of the property.

Back Office Computer. There is presently no stand-alone back office computer. The computers on the property are dated and solely devoted to a property management system that is not Windows based. The following functions could be served with a back office computer:

- Inventory analysis
- Database marketing
- Effective and professional word processing

Parking Lot. The rear parking lot is of particular concern; it does not reflect a three-star property.

Human Resources

The Benson Hotel, like many others before it, had over the years placed people in positions of authority with little or no training to support their efforts. This was true in the following revenue centers.

Dining Room. During high season the dining room enjoys record covers on many nights. However, there was one very stressful situation observed. The staffing was mixed with senior staff followed by poorly trained "warm bodies." The situation was made worse by the supervisor, Rachel, who was perceived by the staff as unfair, unapproachable, and often playing favorites with her friends and family. Rachel, in all fairness, has had no training and was clearly not the person for the job. She repeatedly showed disrespect for her fellow workers and kitchen staff. Unfairness was clearly displayed in the allotment of high-gratuity-paying work such as banquets and bus tours. Rachel played favorites. She would schedule herself and friends to serve high-gratuity events. If you were not her favorite, you were relegated to breakfast shifts or similar low-gratuity work. An example is the new girl, Donna, who Rachel hired this summer. Rachel is already giving preferential shifts to Donna over Isabel, who has been at the Benson for more than five years. Rachel based her decision on Isabel's poor performance, which Rachel said other employees would agree with. This was not the case when fellow workers were asked. Rachel had also threatened to lay off Isabel in the slow months instead of Donna or Rachel's daughter Lucy. This was clearly an old management style and unacceptable in any operation. Rachel is also resentful that the kitchen receives 25 percent of group meal gratuities. In her opinion they do not deserve it. This feeling has permeated among her allies, instilling an "us against them" animosity between the kitchen and service staff.

Kitchen Operation. The kitchen staff is competent, but leadership is seriously lacking in this area. James, the interim kitchen supervisor, has difficulty coping with the restricted responsibilities placed on him and often projects these feelings onto fellow staff. This attitude also has a further negative effect on Rachel and her staff in the dining room. Chef Wilhelm left three months ago and provided little incentive for James to perform his duties as sous-chef. James is somewhat adrift, constantly complaining that he is doing a chef's job and receiving cook's pay.

Management controls and reporting such as inventory are inaccurate at best, with related reports poorly presented (see section concerning the back office computer). Production and food handling require improvement from a quality and sanitation point of view. It seems that many foods taken out for preparation or serving then are left out in a hot kitchen to deteriorate or go to waste. Scheduling of kitchen employees does not seem to relate to business peaks and valleys. This has resulted in calling in casual kitchen staff on short notice, resulting in paid-outs over the counter. One such employee is Gerald, the dishwasher, who is Lucy's boyfriend. Rachel on occasion has taken it upon herself to call Gerald in for dishwashing duty when clearly it is James's responsibility to make the call. This situation provides an opportunity for Rachel to extend her influence beyond the realm of her authority and has led to increased friction between Rachel and James.

Employee Audit

This part of Jim's report was a detailed employee audit interviewing employees on issues from the parking lot all the way up to the general manager. It provided Mike with some food for thought. Jim's opening comments was: "If I had to make only one general statement about the relationship between the employer and employees at this time, I would have to say that it is limping along at a slow, steady pace. Most of the employees appear satisfied with the type of work they are doing and they speak well for the company." Under the section "Lack of Credibility on the Part of the General Manager," Mike's worst fears were confirmed. Jim's report continued, "As far as the remainder of the employees are concerned, they do what they have to and then ignore the general manager. His level of credibility with these employees is zero. One employee was very philosophical about it when she said, "At least we know what we have to deal with, and we are learning how to deal with him. If they get rid of him we could get someone worse." Supporting comments from employees included:

- The general manager is always right.
- The morale of the employees varies with the moods of the general manager.
- The general manager intimidates some employees.

- The general manager tries to impress the upper management by pitching in to help when they are here, but when they are not here he doesn't lift a finger.

Jim summed up this section of his report to Mike like this: "This is a case of employees working well in spite of the general manager rather than because of him. The main problem with this situation is that a reputable company such as the Benson Hotel cannot support the actions of a general manager with this type of comportment and still maintain a workable relationship with its employees. My opinion at this point is that something has to change."

Questions

1. One of the guidelines in transformational leadership is to develop a clear and appealing vision. "Before followers will make a commitment to radical change, they need to have a vision of a better future that is attractive enough to justify the costs of changing familiar ways of doing things." (Yukl 1994) With this in mind, what steps should Mike take immediately to solve the leadership crisis at the Benson Hotel?
2. Do you feel it was necessary for Mike to commission a consultant's report on the Benson? Why or why not? How would you have approached the situation?
3. Identify and propose solutions for the supervisory challenges in the kitchen and dining areas of the Benson Hotel.

References

Yukl, G. 1994. *Leadership in organizations*. Upper Saddle River, N.J.: Prentice Hall.

Labor Productivity

A Hotel Case Study

Objectives

At the completion of this case study, students should be able to:

1. Understand the importance of labor cost and productivity management.
2. Understand some of the key issues important to hotel managers in controlling labor cost.
3. Understand the levels of savings in labor costs achievable with state-of-the-art information and communication technology (ICT).
4. Recognize best practice in hospitality technology approaches.

Case Study Narrative

Labor productivity is a hot hospitality sector topic. British Hospitality Association Chief Executive Bob Cotton was recently quoted, "Unless hospitality businesses maximize productivity, labor shortages, with the resulting rise in labor costs, will continue to be their weakest link." As shown in Figure 1, labor is the biggest cost in the hospitality sector and is increasing steadily.

In 2000, Eproductive Ltd. teamed up with the Inter-Continental Hotels Group to develop a specialist labor scheduling system, *Eproductive Scheduling,* designed to meet the particular needs of this diverse hotel group and, in doing so, the general needs of the majority of the hospitality sector.

Following implementation of *Eproductive Scheduling,* Inter-Continental Hotels Group's Regional Director of Finance, Lars Eldekvist, stated, "Development and implementation of the *Eproductive Scheduling* system and process

Figure 1   Hospitality Industry Key Ratios

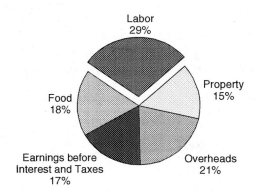

has been demonstrated to make significant improvements to the productivity and costs of our labor."

Project Objectives

The project had three key objectives in the Inter-Continental Hotels Group. The first objective concerned ease of use and cost visibility. The system was able to demonstrate that the application is simple to use and gives visibility to this key cost area. The second objective concerned productivity improvements. The system was able to demonstrate that productivity improvements of 5 percent were achievable in the key departments of food and beverage and housekeeping. The third objective concerned return on investment. The system was able to demonstrate that the project cost could be recovered in less than one year through labor productivity gains and cost savings made.

Results

Implementation of the system for the Inter-Continental Hotels Group was tracked, and results were recorded for the key objectives.

Ease of Use and Cost Visibility

The application was well received. The following is an extract from a report written by a hotel financial controller:

Eproductive Scheduling has empowered the department heads to take ownership of their departmental sales and labor forecasting, making them more aware of correctly recording hours, breaks, sickness, and holidays. The advantages of being able to look at any schedule, at any time, without hunting around for paperwork are significant and looking back at past records is now so easy. We have built *Eproductive Scheduling* into our weekly routine, looking at both past week and current week reports, giving managers the opportunity to amend them, share staff, and control forecast costs. The system has made everyone much more aware of our payroll issues and given us the tools to control it better.

Productivity Improvements

The cost/benefit analysis is based on the benefits achieved in one hotel's house-keeping department. The following approach was adopted:

- A housekeeping department was selected for comparison in this study since the tasks undertaken were the easiest to compare year on year.
- "Rooms cleaned per productive hour" was agreed on as the key indicator for analysis of labor productivity.

Please note that a productive hour does not include nonproductive scheduling types such as holidays, training, or absences. The weekly labor productivity for the full 24-week study period was then plotted and the trend line charted (see Figure 2).

The productivity achieved in rooms cleaned per productive hour increased from an average of 1.6 prior to the implementation of *Eproductive Scheduling* to an average of 1.9 rooms by the end of the period. The target benchmark of 2.0 rooms cleaned per productive hour was also achieved by the end of the period.

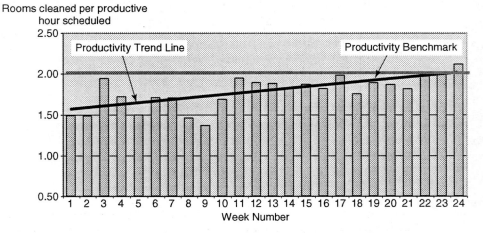

Figure 2   Housekeeping Rooms Cleaned per Productive Hour

Table 1 Housekeeping Department Productivities

	Base line	Achieved
Total Annual Room Nights	27,375	27,375
Total Productive Hours	71.1k	14.5k
Total Staff Cost	£85.5k	£72.4k
Annual Saving vs Base line	n/a	£13.1k
Savings percent	n/a	15.2%
Productivity Gain	1.6	1.89

Table 1 shows the annualized savings available in the housekeeping department alone of £13,100 on the demonstrated productivity improvements. These are based on a hotel with 125 rooms running at an average 60 percent occupancy.

Return on Investment

Eproductive Scheduling is normally provided on an application service provider (ASP) basis. Users pay a fee for each full-time equivalent (FTE) employee scheduled per month. The full implementation costs will vary according to the unit infrastructure in place and the level of training required. Based on the given results, the total hotel implementation costs can be recovered in less than one year by savings made in the housekeeping department alone. There are also opportunities for productivity improvements in other areas where labor flexibility exists, particularly the food and beverage department, which accounts for more than 50 percent of the total hours scheduled in many hotels.

The following indirect benefits were also identified:

- Standardization of scheduling processes
- Ready availability of data with relevant reporting output
- Team focus on labor issues
- Absence and holiday management
- Contribution to due diligence procedures
- Cluster- and company-wide reporting on productivity and cost benchmarks, leading to best practice across the business
- Achieving "right staff, right place, right time," thereby helping to ensure the achievement of brand standards

Note on System Architecture

The *Eproductive Scheduling* software is built on to the flexible core system architecture developed by Eproductive Ltd. *Eproductive Scheduling* is based entirely on a thin-client architecture using open standards including HTTP, XML, and

XSL ensuring extremely rapid deployment and trouble-free integration. It takes advantage of the very latest web-based technology to provide multilevel access to a single Sybase database from any computer with an Internet connection. A key feature is that management at all levels can access the system to enter or retrieve relevant data and reports across their area on labor costs, productivity, and the achievement of brand benchmarks.

Questions

1. Before the development of more effective ICT-based tools, why was it difficult for hotels to schedule labor effectively?
2. In a Housekeeping department, what elements have to be considered when looking at hourly productivity?
3. With what other hotel ICT could labor scheduling systems, such as *Eproductive Scheduling,* be integrated? Review some Internet hospitality websites such as www.WiredHotelier.com and www.HotelResource.com to help you formulate your answer, giving examples of some specific ICT products.

Partnership Marketing

The Forte Hotels Exemplar

Objectives

At the completion of this case study, students should be able to:

1. Define a partnership.
2. List the reasons to create a partnership.
3. Select appropriate partners for an organization given criteria.

Background on Partnerships

Partnerships and Strategic Alliances

> Partnership marketing can be defined as a collaboration of marketing talent, money and ideas when two (or more) companies act as a team in their marketing efforts. They advertise together, set up displays in trade shows together and even send out joint direct marketing. This allows cost reductions and it is especially beneficial for those companies who have products or services that work well together. (Turano 1996)

Today's battles are for customer loyalty and profitability based on efficiency and superior value delivery. As firms develop their strategic vision, they need to develop partnerships with present and potential customers, suppliers, distributors, and competitors.

Attracting Partners

Partnerships can be used to bring together groups not previously allied with or even aware of each other. A partnership is best served when one of the goals of the partnership is to strengthen all of its parts. To accomplish this goal means joint

This case is based on a project conducted by Hsu and Sun in 1996 in conjunction with the Forte group.

53

ownership of the partnership, reciprocation, social obligation, shared wealth, and direct involvement by all groups. Attracting a partner is often most difficult at the beginning when organizations cannot conceptualize why the partnership would benefit them. The forms of a partnership are varied and depend on the intent, goals, and objectives of the partnership. According to Hsu and Sun (1996), the reasons for a partnership are:

- To create synergy by joining efforts
- The pooling of resources
- Escalating competition
- Access to new customers by exchange of customer database
- Partners' leverage expertise
- To satisfy changing customer tastes and preferences
- To create added value for customers.

Common Forms of Partnership Marketing

Organizations have various options for partnerships. Airlines, hotels, credit card companies, car rental companies, and phone companies often form partnerships. To recognize and reward their most loyal customers, airlines created frequent flyer travel award programs. These programs now have become a major marketing force, with large, worldwide membership. An increasing number of hotel partnerships with airlines, long-distance carriers, and even restaurant chains have created new opportunities to earn miles or points without even getting on a plane.

Hotels also may form a partnership with a tourist office. In the future, the trend is to sell not the hotel in a city, but the city first, in other words, the destination. For example, the Connecticut Hotel-Motel Association changed its name to the Connecticut Lodging and Attractions Association following the creation of a strategic alliance with visitors' attractions within the state. Programs such as "*Discover New England*" promote a region with money gathered from all entities of the travel industry.

Consortia. Hotel companies are also joining with travel agency consortia such as American Express Travel Services, Carlson Wagonlit, BTI, and others, for their well-covered, globalized distribution network.

Case Study Narrative

Forte Hotels

Forte Hotels operates many hotels worldwide. It is one of the world's leading hotel and restaurant companies. Despite Forte's well-covered networks in North America and Europe, the chain does not have extensive representation in the

Asia Pacific Region. Potential guests in the newly explored regions generally know nothing or little about the Forte Group. Joining with appropriate partners allows access to partners' leverage and, therefore, maximizes marketing efforts.

The Forte Group acquired Le Méridien Hotels and Resorts. Le Méridien, at the time of purchase, had 53 hotels with 16,500 rooms in more than 40 destinations. This merger was generally regarded as complimentary to Forte Grand properties in terms of product and destination. Le Méridien strengthened the group's presence in Europe, North America, the Middle East, and, for the first time, in the important emerging markets of Asia Pacific.

Summaries of Findings for Le Méridien Hotels and Resorts

Lack of familiarity (44 percent unfamiliar), low advertising awareness (9 percent), and low incidence of usage (13 percent) are unfavorable factors contributing to Le Méridien's poor performance in a rating survey (see Table 1). Among the thirty-two hotel groups surveyed (including major groups such as Hyatt, Sheraton, Hilton, Shangri-La, and Holiday Inn), Le Méridien ranked among the bottom third against most image dimensions. Le Méridien's best-performing attribute was, "They have great resort hotels." They were ranked sixth largely due to respondents' image of Le Méridien, Phuket.

For selecting a business hotel, a hotel's tie with airline and credit card companies was ranked the seventh most important factor (32 percent of absolute variance) after location, past experience, reputation, value for money, availability of business centers, and the presence of high tech equipment in the hotel. In choosing leisure hotels, again, ties with airline and credit card companies were quite important (ranked eighth with 29 percent approvals). The study participants highly valued frequent guest programs (ranked tenth with 18 percent approvals).

Table 1   Perceptions of Respondents Toward Méridien Hotels in Selected Areas as Compared with 31 Major Groups in the Region

Statement	Ranking
They have an excellent reputation	26
One of Asia's very best groups	27
They have beautiful hotels	23
They are well known for service	31
One of my favorites	23
They offer good values for money	25
They have good restaurants	22
They cater to the business traveler	30

Source: Hsu & Sun, 1996.

Forte Goals and Objectives to Be Achieved Through Partnerships

The Forte Group had specific goals and objectives for partnership marketing, especially in the Southeast Asia marketplace.

1. Maximize impacts of limited marketing budgets by increasing customer awareness toward the brands of Forte and Le Méridien Hotels and Resorts.
2. Allow the group's offer to be in line with other rivals by augmenting the range of perks and benefits available to customers, creating a selection of more competitive frequent guest loyalty programs.
3. Attract new customers to generate additional revenues and customer database through effective utilization of partners' databases.
4. Raise customer awareness of brands and hotels by taking advantage of a partner's reputation or other comparative advantages.
5. Positive association of Forte brands alongside national and international brands to maximize customers' brand awareness.
6. Strengthen relationships with partners by establishing strong marketing links.
7. Extend representation regionally and globally through consideration of strategic alliances with quality, noncompetitive hotel chains for partnership marketing and reservations' management. (Hsu and Sun 1996)

The critical issues of a partnership often focus on the maintenance of that partnership. It is important to focus on planning an agreement that benefits everyone, to maintain a strong communication link between the organizations, and to establish evaluation criteria when the partnership is being formed. Partnerships can determine the success of a project by acting as the glue that brings diverse entities together for a common goal. A key to this success is the evaluation process, which must be shared and planned from the beginning of the partnership agreement. Partnership agreements should be assembled so that the group or a member of the group can monitor ground rules, resolve disputes, finance effectively, manage against timetables, and support individual interests as well as the interests of the whole group. The evaluation stage of a partnership should be ongoing.

Partnerships are an integral part of hospitality and tourism development and will continue to be so in the future. Relationship or partnership marketing has three key elements:

1. Identifies and builds a database of current and potential consumers that records and cross-references a wide range of demographics, life-styles, and purchase information.
2. Delivers differentiated messages to these people through established, as well as new, media channels based on customers' characteristics and preferences.

3. Tracks each relationship to monitor the cost of acquiring the customers and the lifetime value of their purchases.

As companies are shifting their marketing dollars from mass media to more targeted and more measurable forms of advertising, they are taking advantage of relationship marketing. Strong marketing programs are essential to create and maintain a solid customer base, as well as to bring new customers into the Forte Hotel system. The group might also encourage and closely monitor cross-utilization of databases between respective divisions. To maximize the power of relationship marketing, the group could build alliances with partners that could extend access to additional target market clusters and offer indispensable data used to tailor effective marketing programs.

Question

Given the group's goals and objectives, what are some recommended strategies in Asia for the Forte Group?

References

Hsu, W. and S. Sun, 1996. *Partnership marketing: A global growth strategy.* Report to Forte International. Hong Kong.

Turano, J., 1996. Member Forum, American Marketing Association, http://www.ama.org.

Hotel Recruitment
in a Rural Environment

Making Lemonade from Lemons

Objectives

At the completion of this case study, students should be able to:

1. Estimate unmet business demand for an area.
2. Assume and estimate induced demand for a new property in a town of this size.
3. Project new demand from the property's year round operation.
4. Suggest possible new markets for a property.
5. Determine whether a project is actually feasible.

Case Study Narrative

How can the town of Ticonderoga, with a population of only 5,000 and in the absence of demand for a full-service lodging facility, entice a lodging facility to come in and support Fort Ticonderoga's desire to be a year-round visitor destination? The Fort will need sleeping rooms, meeting rooms, and food and beverage facilities to support its plan for year-round operations; thus, the new facility must be a full-service property. A 100- to 150-room lodging property might be economically feasible. A standard "rule of thumb" cost for such a property will be used to estimate economic success.

New lodging support is required for the Fort's year-round plans. The year-round operations from the Fort currently are not sufficient to justify a new lodging property; therefore, the Fort's demand must be augmented by other means to justify such a property.*

Background Information

Ticonderoga, New York, is a small town of approximately 5,000 people located at the northern tip of Lake George. Approximately 70 miles north of Ticonderoga is the largest population center of the three-county upstate New York area—Plattsburgh, New York—with a population of approximately 30,000, including approximately 6,000 students at Plattsburgh State University. To the south of Ticonderoga and on the southern tip of Lake George is the Village of Lake George. Lake George is located within Adirondack State Park, the largest state park in the United States. The Adirondack State Park is a beautiful geographic area of over 6 million acres and includes within its boundaries the entire Adirondack mountain range. In addition, the region has a rich history, especially concerning the early settlement of the area, transportation routes, the French and Indian War, and the Revolutionary War.

The upstate area has three distinctive tourism seasons. Summer, or the traditional tourism season, is very strong due to the history, the climate, the mountains, and the various recreational aspects of Lake George and Lake Champlain, a much larger lake located a few miles north of Lake George. The summer season is mostly family travel, focused around the history, geography, and the recreational attributes of the region. Fall or foliage season is the second draw, as the "leaf peepers" visit the area to view some of the most magnificent fall foliage colors anywhere. This not only attracts a family market, but is enhanced by large numbers of bus charters. These charters market to a wide variety of groups including photographers, naturalists, elderly travelers, young adults, and families, as well as offering educational tours. The highways are thick with visitors during the fall foliage season. The winter season is specifically for ski and winter sports recreation. The center for winter visitation is around the Village of Lake Placid, located approximately 80 miles northwest of the Lake George area. Lake Placid is a growing area and is attempting to become more of a year-round tourism town. However, its image and operations are still focused around its history as home to the 1980 Winter Olympics. Thus, in the upstate area there is a strong tourism market both for summer and winter visitation, making it a destination tourism area. However, within the upstate destination area, there is no single town or attraction that can be considered the primary destination point. The area is currently a "touring" or "pass through" region, meaning visitors pass in and around many varied sites and communities with no one community or site having a true dominance.

*This case study is based on a feasibility study prepared for Lakes To Locks Passage, Inc., Crown Point, New York, by the Technical Assistance Center (TAC), Plattsburgh State University, School of Business and Economics, Plattsburgh, New York. TAC is funded in part by the U.S. Department of Commerce, Economic Development Administration, University Center program.

Since the population of the largest community is only about 25,000 (without students), the vast majority of lodging facilities in the upstate region are small mom-and-pop operations. The summer attractions generally close for the winter, such as Fort Ticonderoga, all water recreation areas, and most hotels and lodging facilities. Some museums close, while others remain open but reduce visitation hours.

Ticonderoga has a total of fewer than 100 rooms supplied by four operations. Only Lake Placid and Plattsburgh have full-service, mid- or upscale national brands of lodging. Historically, the upstate area has had specific communities for each of the three tourism seasons (summer, fall, and winter). The Fort management expects to have a number of educational conferences, workshops, and exhibits during the late fall, winter, and early spring months that would require attendees to stay overnight. These visitors will add substantially to the 100,000 visitors the Fort currently attracts in its summer season, but they will require a new lodging facility of at least 100 rooms to service those visitors, including sleeping rooms, conference and meeting space, and food and beverage facilities.

Financial Norms for the Lodging Industry

In all hotel development, planners should establish the economic feasibility of the hotel. A commonly accepted rule of thumb in the lodging industry for gauging hotel development is that one dollar of daily rate room revenue must be realized per each thousand dollars spent to construct a sleeping room, given two-thirds occupancy. Currently, a typical mid-scale full-service property has an average room construction cost of $75,000. Thus, the following can be assumed:

Hotel rooms	Available room-nights	Average required minimum occupancy	Room-nights sold for break-even	Total room revenue at $75 average daily rate
100	36,500 (365×100)	66%	24,090	$1.8 Million
150	54,750 (365×150)	66%	36,135	$2.7 Million

The goal is to find a minimum of 24,090 nights during 12 months.

Market Information for Area

There is little reliable tourism data from the upstate region, not to mention the Ticonderoga market specifically. Other sources of data were found providing guidance and giving the following information:

- The range of occupancy reported for New York (outside of New York City) is a high greater than 90 percent, and a low of approximately 40 percent. The average is 60 percent.
- This range reflects a high during the summer season (June, July, August) and the foliage season (approximately October) and a low for the "mud season"

(March, April, May). Winter season can include a strong month depending on weather and snow conditions.

- National hotel surveys show an average annual occupancy and an average daily rate for mid-scale properties at 59.8 percent and $72.

- A nonscientific survey of the region by the researchers via phone calls to various properties provided the following results: a low end for rooms in the $45 range (mostly independent properties and some budget properties), to a high end of $90 to over $100.

- Examples of specific room rates include a $55 budget chain in Plattsburgh, $69 mid-scale chain in Plattsburgh, $45 independent in Ticonderoga, $55 budget chain in Ticonderoga, $75 to $110 for mid-scale chains in Lake Placid, $55 to over $100 for independents and budget properties in the Lake George area, $79 for a mid-scale chain in Burlington, and a high of $95 for a budget chain in the Catskills.

The following seasonal data were gathered from regional tourism industry personnel:

Summer (June, July, August)	Strong—traditional summer season
September	Slow
October	Strong—foliage season
November	Slow
December	Slow to moderate, with some holiday demand
January to mid-March	Moderate to strong—dependent on snow conditions
March, April, May	Very Slow—mud season

The Fort will not estimate how many actual room nights they may need, but indicates that they expect a significant usage if a new hotel was available. Their preliminary plans are for approximately forty-five new functions during the off season in year one. The number of events should increase in future years. These functions will be anywhere from one day to one week in duration and attract anywhere from 10 to 200 people. Additionally, International Paper Company (IP), the town's only large industry, indicates it has a significant number of business travelers in and out of the town on a regular basis. The regional Visitors and Conventions Bureau estimates that about 10 visitors to the plant per day currently need overnight accommodations. Plant officials also confirmed that many monthly plant meetings would be held locally if meeting space were available. In addition, two steamboats operate out of the Village of Lake George and travel to the north end of Lake George from May to September. The steamboats do not stop at Ticonderoga unless prior arrangements have been made.

Questions

1. What occupancy level would you assume for a 100- to 150-room hotel, and during what seasons, based on general occupancy information for New York and general occupancy levels nationally?

2. Propose some additional (logical) actions the town could possibly take to increase the visitor demand for this property?

3. Given the inexact information in the case, what would be a reasonable assumption to make regarding room nights from the Fort's expanded (year-round) operations and from International Paper's business?

4. Given all the information developed and analyzed, is it logical for a developer to build either a 100-room or a 150-room property in this town?

5. Would it be logical for the town to offer any economic incentives to help encourage a new lodging property?

Franchise Services Evaluation

Objectives

At the completion of the case study, students should be able to:

1. Identify the value of franchise services provided by franchise companies.
2. Analyze a franchise package for its potential worth.

Case Study Narrative

Determining the return on investment (ROI) for hotel management companies is a difficult task. ROI in this context refers to the services provided by the franchiser for the monies paid and the quality of those services perceived by hotel general managers. A large hotel management company with more than 33,000 rooms offering premier, full-service, and economy lodging to more than five million guests annually was interested in getting more return for their investment with franchisers. Their organization was examined to yield the following discussion.

Franchisers and Franchisees

While recognition can be created through advertising and promotion, one of the best methods of developing a known hotel brand name is to have a product for people to see and use (Rushmore 1990). The entire franchise package has value, particularly the established consumer image and goodwill, and especially to an independent hotel in need of identity and image. Hotel franchisees want more from franchisers (Baum 1994). This is the prevailing attitude of most franchisees.

Franchisees want state-of-the-art reservation systems, technology, marketing, purchasing, and training; they want the franchiser to produce more profit (Baum 1994). Hotel owners or management companies change brands to take advantage of better name recognition, reservation systems, and marketing support (Baum 1994). Owners are looking at franchisers more critically than in the past, seeing who can deliver more business for them (Baum 1994).

The costs of selecting an incorrect franchise can be great. Hotel franchise fees are the compensation paid to the franchiser for the use of the chain's name, logo, identity, image, good will, procedures and controls, marketing, and referral and reservation systems (Rushmore and Duffy 1996). An investment of this magnitude by any management company or owner requires careful consideration.

Data Collection

Research of secondary data concerning franchises and franchise services, including internal operating statistics and call reports (similar to telephone surveys), was conducted to generate categories for evaluation in the surveys to be administered to hotel general managers. General managers and sales managers for all the franchises in the company were contacted. Based on the data collected, thirty-four services and franchiser programs were listed for evaluation. These services and programs were then categorized into four areas: marketing, education and training, other services, and reservations.

A survey was developed and distributed to all general managers and sales managers. Fifty-two surveys were distributed and thirty-four returned, yielding a 65.4 percent return rate. The managers were asked to rate franchiser services and programs on a scale of 1 (least valuable) to 5 (most valuable). The results of the survey are illustrated in Tables 1 and 2, Manager Perceptions of Franchise Services and Programs, Aggregated Rankings, and Manager Perceptions of Programs and Services: Ranking by Hotel Chain. The tabulated results are presented in aggregated form, presenting a generalized interpretation of franchise products and services.

The perceptions of hotel general managers and sales managers are important to evaluate a franchise and the selection of a brand affiliation. Franchisers offer many services and programs. Franchisees, however, are looking for the best and correct match for their product. Some of the results were expected and are understandable. For example, when a hotel relies on a reservation system for its business, that system is clearly an important program. A Holiday Inn franchise, for example, is more focused on the use of Holidex to generate its room-night demand.

Services like food and beverage standards and other related programs might not be applicable to all hotels. Rooms-only properties or hotel management companies with their own food and beverage departments and standards have little use for these types of services. Some level of duplication exists between the services

Table 1   Manager Perceptions of Franchiser Services and Programs: Aggregated Rankings

	Mean	Standard Deviation
Marketing		
National advertising	3.647	1.041
National sales/marketing	3.353	1.051
Travel agent promotions	3.029	1.070
Seasonal franchise promotions	2.971	1.080
Frequent guest programs	2.824	1.087
Regional marketing support	2.824	1.087
Group sales	2.818	1.122
S.T.A.R. Reports	2.735	1.218
Airline promotions	2.735	1.228
Co-op advertising	2.636	1.238
Trade show representation	2.500	1.243
Access to lead database	2.485	1.245
Stock advertising	2.485	1.261
In-house merchandising	2.471	1.460
Brochure and collateral production	2.294	1.507
In-room/food collateral	2.029	1.586
Telemarketing	1.794	1.601
Education/Training		
Franchise conferences/seminars	3.118	1.094
Employee educational programs	3.059	1.205
Training manuals	2.882	1.403
Training for new employees	2.824	1.409
Special programs for general manager	2.824	1.466
Orientation for new employees	2.706	1.477
Sales training	2.618	1.488
Other Services		
Standard inspections	3.382	1.206
Guest evaluations	3.000	1.256
Negotiated vendor contracts	2.765	1.257
Regional operations supervisor	2.471	1.382
Customer focus groups	2.382	1.482
Provided furniture/fixtures/renovations	2.344	1.497
Food and beverage standards	2.152	1.562
Matching funds for renovations	1.382	1.776
Reservations		
Reservations system	3.938	1.014
Franchise service coordinator	3.194	1.276

**Table 2   Manager Perceptions of Franchiser Services and Programs:
Ranking By Hotel Chain**

	A	B	C	D	E	F
Service or Program	**Mean**	**Mean**	**Mean**	**Mean**	**Mean**	**Mean**
National sales/marketing	3.09	3.25	3.50	4.40	3.67	1.67
National advertising	3.09	3.50	4.50	4.20	3.67	3.00
Co-op advertising	1.80	3.00	2.67	3.80	3.00	2.00
Brochure and collateral production	1.27	2.25	3.67	2.20	4.00	1.67
Trade show representation	1.73	2.50	3.17	2.60	3.00	2.33
Travel agent promotions	2.27	2.75	3.17	3.60	3.67	3.33
Airline promotions	2.00	2.00	2.67	3.20	3.67	3.33
Seasonal franchise promotions	2.45	3.00	3.50	4.00	3.00	2.67
Telemarketing	1.18	1.25	2.33	2.00	3.00	2.67
Access to lead database	1.50	2.00	2.83	4.80	3.33	3.67
In-house merchandising	2.18	1.25	2.83	2.60	3.67	3.00
S.T.A.R. reports	1.55	2.25	2.83	3.80	4.33	4.33
Group sales	2.00	2.75	2.83	4.60	3.33	2.00
Stock advertising	1.91	1.75	2.50	3.40	3.33	2.33
Frequent guest programs	1.55	2.00	3.33	4.60	3.33	3.33
In-room/food collateral	1.82	1.50	2.17	2.20	3.00	2.00
Regional marketing support	2.45	2.50	2.67	3.40	3.67	2.33
Franchise conferences/ seminars	2.64	3.50	3.00	3.80	4.00	2.33
Training manuals	2.09	3.75	3.17	3.00	3.67	2.33
Employees educational programs	2.45	3.25	3.33	3.20	4.33	2.33
Training for new employees	2.00	3.25	2.83	3.60	4.33	1.67
Orientation for new employees	2.09	2.50	2.67	3.40	4.33	2.00
Special programs for general manager	1.82	4.00	2.83	3.40	4.00	2.33
Sales training	1.64	2.75	3.33	2.60	4.33	2.33
Food and beverage Standards	1.40	1.75	2.83	2.60	3.33	3.00
Negotiated vendor contracts	2.36	2.25	3.17	3.60	3.00	2.67
Customer focus groups	1.73	2.50	2.67	3.00	3.00	2.33
Standard inspections	2.82	3.50	2.83	4.20	4.33	3.00
Provided furniture/fixtures/ renovations	2.30	3.25	2.17	2.00	1.67	1.50
Guest evaluations	2.00	3.50	2.83	3.80	4.33	2.33
Matching funds for renovations	1.45	1.50	2.67	1.00	2.00	1.67
Regional operations supervisor	1.91	3.25	2.00	1.60	4.33	3.00
Franchise service coordinator	2.70	3.50	2.50	3.40	4.33	3.33
Reservations system	3.50	3.25	4.00	4.80	4.33	3.67

provided by hotel management companies and franchisers. However, from the hotel management company perspective, if it is to include the cost of a franchise on its profit and loss statement, the franchiser needs to create value for the price.

Franchisers might think about their programs and services in comparison to insurance benefits offered by an organization to its employees. If a company offers a tuition reimbursement program but the employee has no interest in going to school, there is little perceived value in the benefit. Similarly, if a franchiser offers services not needed by the hotel, the value of those services is small. Therefore, franchisers might be better positioned if they offered a portfolio or menu of choices. Some programs might be standards, such as a reservation and national advertising system, but others could be selected or declined.

Conclusion

For a hotel management company this research serves as an evaluation tool for the sales and marketing department. Further elaboration of these data will assist a hotel management company in determining the return on investment for each franchise. Better information and collaboration between potential franchisees and franchisers could produce better matches of brand and product and increased value for all.

Questions

1. What does the data indicate and what services are most important? Why?
2. What does all this mean to an owner reviewing potential franchises?
3. What is the best value and how can one determine the best selection of brands?
4. If you were in charge of selecting brand names for your properties, what would this information mean to you?

The Madison Hotel
in Memphis

A Case Study in the Creation
and Development of a Boutique Hotel

Objective

At the completion of this case study, students should be able to outline the hotel development and renovation process including: parcel assembly, permanent financing, investment tax credits and related financial incentives, and business entity formation, as well as debt, equity, and deal structuring.

Case Study Narrative

This case study focuses on the experiences of four developer/entrepreneurs and the lessons they learned in the creation of a 110-unit luxury European style boutique hotel in downtown Memphis, Tennessee. The hotel project was conceived in 1995 and culminated seven years later with the grand opening of Memphis' only boutique hotel on May 1, 2002. This discussion also provides insight into the complexities of hotel renovation projects and provides some things to watch out for those who may become involved in the development of a similar hotel as either an entrepreneur or a team member in a corporate setting.

The Players

The individuals identified in this case study are:

- Walter Broadfoot, a veteran hotel developer/owner and broker from Memphis whose career was spawned during the halcyon days of Kemmons Wilson and the Holiday Inns Broadfoot developed Holiday Inns throughout the mid-south, midwest, and northeast.

- Tony Klok and Gene Kornota of Chicago investors who funded the majority of the equity for the project from the proceeds of three small boutique hotels they sold just before they got involved in the Madison.
- Mohamad Hakimian the long-time general manager of Memphis' most famous hotel, the Peabody, who became involved in the project after its initial conception. As a managing partner he was instrumental in shaping the renovation and character of the hotel.

The Initial Concept

Walter Broadfoot first eyed the Tennessee Trust Building in 1995 as a possible boutique hotel while looking down on it from the twenty-second floor of his attorney's office in downtown Memphis. Since the Hotel Peabody was downtown's only four-star lodging facility, and it was achieving respectable market performance, Broadfoot began to ponder the idea of a boutique hotel for the Tennessee Trust Building. There were many questions that went through Broadfoot's mind, not the least of which was whether the Memphis lodging market had enough depth and average rate potential to support a boutique hotel and the challenges of acquiring and renovating a shuttered property in a historic preservation district. Undaunted, as most entrepreneurs are by such a challenge, it wasn't very long before Broadfoot began to dig in and pursue his first boutique hotel opportunity in earnest. As he looks back, Broadfoot now concedes that had he known then what he knows now, namely the complexity and extent of the challenges that faced him, he would have abandoned the project right then and there.

The Tennessee Trust Building

The Tennessee Trust Building, which opened in 1906, was an almost ideal structure to convert to a hotel because each of its original offices had a window and an identical floor plan from floors three through sixteen, a large ground floor lobby, a second-level mezzanine, a lower or basement level, and the potential for a rooftop deck that would command a breathtaking view of the mighty Mississippi, located only several hundred yards from the property. However, the property lacked any additional space for food, beverage, and banquet facilities.

Acquisition Challenges

As Broadfoot puts it, "Before you get involved in the purchasing of a property like the Tennessee Trust Building, you can't begin to know the extent of the problems you will encounter." As an example, CNA Insurance Company, which was selling the building, had acquired it from the defunct Fireman's Fund Insurance for $250,000. However, CNA didn't even hold legal title to it because it was still in the name of the previous company that had owned it. Broadfoot had to file papers to bankrupt the former company and then purchase it "on the courthouse steps" out of bankruptcy. This unplanned process took several months out of Broadfoot's development schedule. After many months of real estate entanglements and expenses that skyrocketed to over $100,000 involving architects, engineers, and attorneys, Broadfoot bought the building for $325,000. Sound like a bargain? Read on.

Parcel Assembly

In addition to Broadfoot's purchase of the Tennessee Trust Building, three additional properties had to be acquired in order to make space for the hotel's food, beverage and banquet facilities. Table 1 depicts the various buildings that were acquired and several related specifics.

As Broadfoot began to assemble the adjacent parcels, he encountered owners who were either unwilling to sell or wanted to make a "quick buck" when they realized that a developer wanted to acquire their property for a hotel. As an example, one of the parcels in the assembly recently had been purchased for $150,000 but had to be bought several months later by Broadfoot at a considerable premium over its recent acquisition price.

The Development Budget

After many months of planning and meetings, a development budget was prepared indicating a total project cost of $9.7 million. By the time the hotel was complete this figure swelled to approximately $15 million or 50 percent more than the original project cost estimate. The developers cite several major factors that drove up the original budget:

- The enhancement of the initial food and beverage concept, which was originally to be limited in scope but evolved into a full-service/upscale grill and bar that would be a distinctive restaurant. (Today with a total of only 52 seats Grill 83 has been positively acclaimed by local restaurant critics and was

Table 1   Property Acquisition Data

Address	Use	Total Square Feet	Acquisition Cost	Cost/ Sq. Ft.	Cost/Room
# 79 Madison	Hotel Tower	89,000	$325,000	$3.65	$2,955
# 83 Madison	Grill 83	3,160	201,700	$63.83	$1,834
# 9 Main St	Function space	2,600	225,000	$86.54	$2,045
# 11 Main St.	Function space	2,600	248,000	$95.38	$2,255
Totals/Average	n/a	97,360	$999,700	$10.27	$9,088

Table 2   Project Development Costs

Item	Amount	Cost/Sq. Ft.	Cost/Room
Building acquisition cost	$ 999,700	$ 10.06	$ 9,088
Construction cost	10,000,000	100.64	90,909
Architectural and engineering	500,000	5.03	4,545
Furniture, fixtures and equipment	3,000,000	30.19	27,273
Legal, accounting, miscellaneous	300,000	3.02	2,727
Project contingency	255,000	2.57	2,318
Total project cost	$15,054,700	$151.52	$136,861

expected to achieve total annual sales volumes approaching $2.0 million in 2003.)

- Inaccurate and insufficient construction cost budgets prepared by an unqualified general contractor, who among other things failed to take into account that construction labor cost would be driven up because the property had only eight rooms per floor.
- Challenges with the general contractor which required firing the first due to on-time performance issues, and then finding and hiring another firm, which not only delayed the opening of the hotel but drove up the expense from the ensuing construction interest that continued well beyond the time frame that was originally anticipated. The replacement general contractor who was hired, not only agreed to monetary incentives for early completion, but to liquidated damages for failure to complete the project on time. Table 2 illustrates the principal development costs (line items) of the hotel upon its final completion.

Financial Incentives

In 1977, an agency known as the Center City Commission was established by the Memphis City and County government to foster and improve the local economy by leading an aggressive public and private effort to promote the redevelopment and economic growth of the Central Business District. These incentives include low interest loans on borrowings up to $90,000 plus a freeze on property taxes for up to 20 years. For the Madison, the property tax benefit alone amounted to a cost savings of approximately $100,000 per year. However, the biggest and most important financial incentive was the Investment Tax Credit (ITC) which allowed 20 percent of the actual construction cost of $10 million to be given as a tax credit. Stipulations of the program require that the ITC payments be distributed out over a five year period. Since the Madison developers could not take advantage of a $2 million dollar tax credit against their income, they were able to sell their ITC to the local Regions Bank who purchased it for $0.95 on the dollar (making a profit of $100,000) and will make five installments to the limited liability corporation (LLC) in the amount of $380,000 per year.

Table 3   Debt and Equity Structure

Item	Amount (in thousands)	Percentage
Equity	$7.81	52.0
Debt	$7.20	48.0
Total project cost	$15.01	100.0

Tax-Free Exchange Provisions.   Tony Klok and Gene Kornota had recently sold three small hotels in Chicago resulting in potentially significant capital gains tax; however, their proceeds were immediately rolled over into the Madison hotel project, thereby deferring the payment of any capital gains tax through an IRS regulation known as a 1031 tax-free exchange. This provision defers the payment of any capital gains tax as long as the proceeds are rolled over into similar or "like kind" investment and none of the proceeds are distributed as income to the investors.

Bank Financing.   Because of the perceived and real risks of the project, there weren't any local banks interested in providing permanent financing for the project. A loan was finally made by the Republic Bank of Chicago based on the banking relationship of Tony and Gene and on the condition that they be given a second mortgage on another hotel owned by Tony and Gene. As is customary in most hotel's financing arrangements, personal guarantees were required from each partner by the lender. Table 3 depicts the debt and equity structure of the project. As indicated, the Republic Bank of Chicago made a loan on about 50 percent of the project cost and the bank will continue to hold title to the building as additional secured collateral.

Ownership Structure of the LLC

The business entity that was formed to own the hotel was a Tennessee limited liability corporation. Table 4 illustrates the ownership structure. Equity share is defined as the actual cash equity contributed by each partner while the financial share represents the structure of the profit distributions after each partner receives a 12 percent return on their original cash equity. The difference between the equity share and the financial share is the "sweat equity" granted to Walter Broadfoot and General Manager Mohamad Hakimian by principle investors Tony and Gene.

Table 4   Ownership Structure

	Equity Share	Financial Share
Investor # 1	45%	35%
Investor # 2	45%	35%
Investor # 3	5%	15%
Investor # 4	5%	15%

Table 5　Guest Room Configuration

Room Mix	Number	Size (sq. ft.)
Presidential suites	2	600
Hospitality suites	2	240
Superior double	12	312
Deluxe double	14	520
Superior queen/double	16	242
Deluxe king	14	520
Superior king	12	482
King one bedroom suite	38	600
Totals/Average	110	440

The Final Product

The doors of the Madison Hotel opened on May 2, 2002; sixteen months after major demolition and renovations began on the Tennessee Trust Building. Grill 83 Restaurant and the hotel's function space opened on August 16, 2003. Configuration of the hotel's guest rooms and public areas are illustrated in Table 5 and Figure 1.

Rentable units	110
Grill 83 seating	52
Function space seating:	
Classroom seating	150
Banquet seating	130
Board room	14
Mezzanine seating	22
Lobby seating	24
Swimming/Lap pool	50 × 20
Exercise/Fitness area	300 sq. ft.
Rooftop deck/Patio seating	100

Figure 1　Scope of Project

Questions

1. What key issues needed to be addressed in the development and renovation process?
2. What did the developer learn through this process?

Cases in Resort and Club Management

A Fresh Start
at the Rainbow Golf Resort

Objectives

At the completion of the case study, students should be able to:

1. Identify operational concerns involving property transition.
2. Coordinate departmental employee staffing and training.
3. Restructure the organizational chart.

Case Study Narrative

The Rainbow Golf Resort had something to celebrate. The 120-unit golf resort consisting of villas and condominiums had recently been "re-branded" from a franchise to an independent property. The new owner, Ken Okura, was reviewing the present organizational structure of the Rainbow along with the files of key personnel presently running the operation. During the transition period Ken had recruited his own team including a Vice-president of Operations, Director of Sales and Marketing and Director of Food and Beverage to restructure the organization; however, he still had a few key areas to fill in. In the past, each member of the resort's management team had staked out his or her own turf with little internal communication. As a case in point, Ken often noticed Shirley, the accountant, regularly directing the front desk on policies and procedures. All this happened under the watch of Jeremy, the resort's Rooms Division Manager, who didn't seem to take notice of such actions. Ken thought that this overlap of authority surely must confuse the front desk staff.

The transition period had provided Ken with a window of opportunity to evaluate the line and supervisory staff. Ken had retained Ted Barrow, a human resources consultant; his report's findings were quite a surprise to Ken. Ted's report began with the following staff concerns:

- The management does not work together. There is no teamwork, only "flexing" for power. Managers are out to protect their turf. This attitude pervades the resort.
- There is no apparent overall direction for the resort. If there is, it is not being communicated throughout the organization.
- There is no general manager or controller on site. The feeling is that if these people were around, conflict among the department heads could be avoided.
- There is insufficient training. Employees are thrown into their jobs without being ready to perform them properly. They should have proper preparation before they have to deal with guests.
- Some departments (front desk in particular) are terribly understaffed. This causes service problems as well as high staff turnover.
- The staff morale is low. Employees work in separate departments and get caught in a rut. There is no overall team spirit. It's more like "every man for himself."
- There is little or no awareness of how other departments operate. This knowledge is necessary to help us understand how we impact each other.
- Many people are currently unhappy. The labor pool is small, and if they leave it will be tough to replace them. Management should work to keep the staff happy.
- There seems to be a consensus that staff members want to be able to provide good service, but too many constraints are placed on them to be able to do so.
- It is difficult to know who to go to if someone has a problem with his or her manager. There should be someone designated as the resort manager so that employees have someone to communicate with should the need to do so arise.

Ken assembled his new team to map out strategies to address the operational challenges and employee concerns.

Questions

1. Identify and describe four short-term operational strategies Ken should implement immediately at the Rainbow Golf Resort.
2. What human resources and training initiatives should Ken implement at the Rainbow Golf Resort?
3. Which form of top-down communication would be most suitable for the Rainbow Golf Resort to achieve its objectives?
4. Identify some orientation techniques Ken and his team could implement to introduce the employees to the new ownership of the Rainbow Golf Resort.

5. Using the available information, form a detailed and well-argued plan of action for the Rainbow Golf Resort.

Suggested Reading

Depree, M. 1989. *Leadership is an art.* New York: Bantam/Doubleday/Dell Publishing Group Inc.

Gardner, J. 1990. *On leadership.* New York: The Free Press.

Go, F., M. Monachello, and T. Baum. 1996. *Human resource management in the hospitality industry.* New York: John Wiley & Sons.

Kotter, J. 1996. *Leading change.* Boston: Harvard Business School Press.

Kouzes, J., and B. Posner. 1993. *The leadership challenge.* San Francisco: Jossey-Bass.

Lewis, R. 1998. *Cases in hospitality strategy and policy.* New York: John Wiley and Sons.

Marriott, J. W., and K. Brown. 1997. *The spirit to serve Marriott's way.* New York: HarperCollins.

Senge, P. 1990. *The fifth discipline.* New York: Currency Doubleday.

Vaill, P. B. 1996. *Learning as a way of being.* San Francisco: Jossey-Bass.

Yukl, G. 1994. *Leadership in organizations.* Englewood Cliffs NJ: Prentice Hall.

Blue Thistle Country Club

Objectives

At the completion of the case study, students should be able to:

1. Identify and discuss five critical issues requiring immediate attention.
2. Identify and discuss five necessary issues (not critical) to address within six months.
3. Identify and discuss five important issues (important, but not necessary) that should be adopted into the Club philosophy over a period of time.

Case Study Narrative

The Blue Thistle Country Club case presents participants with the opportunity to consider a variety of situations similar to those a general manager would face at an actual club.

Assume you have been hired as a consultant by the owners to analyze the situation. You will provide the board with ideas and prioritized recommendations about problems. Unlike many consultants, you have a vested stake in the matter. Since it is likely the board will change managers, they will consider your recommendations and perhaps select you to carry out such a plan. Therefore, your advice on how to implement your recommendations must be well thought out.

Authors' Note: All events, people, and circumstances in the case are fictitious. Any resemblance to actual clubs, locations, or people in them is coincidental.

Background

The Blue Thistle Country Club was founded in 1927 by the owner of a large Los Angeles railroad company. His purpose was to establish a rural getaway for senior managers and invited employees of the organization. At the time of its founding, the Blue Thistle Country Club consisted of a large bunkhouse (capable of sleeping forty persons) built along the rim of picturesque Tarantula Canyon, which was said to contain abundant wildlife. A 5,000-square-foot lodge housing gathering rooms, a kitchen, and dining space for about eighty people sat atop a natural elevated mound affording a commanding view of the area. Both the bunkhouse and the Lodge were designed by noted architect Lawrence Fremont, in the California-Craftsman style.

The facilities were furnished in camp-style motif—heavy wooden chairs, bunk beds, and large overstuffed couches covered in game bird prints. The bunkhouse contained only four rooms—a large dormitory-style sleeping room, a combination kitchen and chow area, and two large bathrooms with gang showers. Both the bunkhouse and the common space were heated by oil-fired stoves, and water was pumped directly from the canyon stream. The stoves were also used for cooking.

Besides hunting, visitors to the facility could enjoy an eighteen-hole golf course built at the same time as the bunkhouse. Both the retreat and the surrounding property contained large numbers of deer, quail, coyotes, mountain lions, and bears. In total, the property consisted of approximately 5,000 acres of land—most of it arid, desert-quality grassland used for grazing cattle and growing barley. At the time the retreat was built, access to the facilities and grounds was limited to managers and employees of the company.

The rural retreat was located approximately fifty miles south of Los Angeles in the Raptor Mountain foothills. For the first forty-six years (1927–1973), the facility remained essentially as it was when it was built. Minimally maintained by the company, few renovations were attempted on the facilities. The property was used primarily as a rustic, males-only hunting, hiking, and golf retreat. On occasion, the company used the facility for official meetings, but most of the time use was limited to relaxing retreats and casual entertaining.

Over the years, the urban sprawl from Los Angeles grew further and further south toward the facility so that by the mid-1960s many new incorporated cities, including major suburban developments, had extended to within a few miles of the retreat.

As development spread closer to the facility, its usefulness as a retreat declined, and as highways improved throughout the state, more of the company's managers and employees found reasons to go elsewhere to get away from work for a few days. By the time the facility was sold in 1973, most vacationers were more interested in visiting Santa Barbara, San Diego, or other resort towns along the Southern California coast with their families.

In 1973, the facility was sold to a group of investors intent on creating a private golf club within what would become one of the first planned unit developments in order to take advantage of the rapidly increasing participation in golf and, at the same time, to create a high-quality amenity for the marketing of high-end real estate. In the same year, the project was formally named Blue Thistle Country Club and a marketing program began.

Many of the existing facilities of the original property were retained in the new development. However, their use was relegated to housing construction and service workers while they were building and working in the new facility. The bunkhouse continued to be used for the service staff after the new club facility was constructed, and the original lodge building was used for seasonal storage. Upon noticing that the original oil storage tanks had rusted through, the manager directed the maintenance supervisor to junk them. In recent years, on their occasional tours of the property, club managers and employees had found signs of teen parties. The generally held impression was that the lodge was used without permission by local kids and the service staff for occasional beer parties. On one tour, signs of people camping in the old lodge were discovered—a kerosene lantern, blankets, and small ash piles. No Trespassing signs were posted.

The New Facility

The new clubhouse was built on open land well away from the original bunkhouse and lodge. The original eighteen-hole golf course, which ran in links style along the floor of the canyon, was retained in the new development as the North Course, and an additional links-style South Course was added. The clubhouse was located between the two courses. After development of the new facility, the club used only about 500 acres of the total property.

A problem often cited by members was the inability to view either of the two finishing holes from the clubhouse. This was because of a willow field alongside the streambed of the canyon floor that blocked the view. In this part of California, willows are considered a habitat for endangered species. The manager, at the urging of the golf committee, ordered the trees to be thinned over time to improve the view to either of the finishing greens. The golf course superintendent put through a purchase order for two chain saws and said the project would be completed over a thirty-day period and that no one would ever notice what was done; members would gradually just start being able to see the greens.

The Clubhouse

The clubhouse at Blue Thistle Country Club was built in 1973 when the property was bought. The two-story building imitated the architectural style of the original lodge and bunkhouse. The new California-Craftsman building was well accepted throughout the community and featured stained-glass windows, heavy-timbered ceilings, and handcrafted mahogany furniture. The many large windows provided commanding views of the golf courses, pools, and tennis courts.

The facility served as a valuable tool for selling prospects on the community and the club, and it won several design awards. However, seating capacity was limited to less than 150 people, since there was no banquet space. Members eventually became disenchanted and frustrated that the club could not seat an awards banquet for such benchmark functions as the member-guest tournament.

In addition to luxurious mahogany-paneled locker rooms for men and women, the clubhouse had two kitchens, one to serve the main dining room and one to serve the grill and the infamous men's card room. It was thought that men would be the most active at the club and would make the decision to buy the membership or property within the community; therefore, the club was planned to cater to men. The men's locker room was approximately three times the size of the women's and included lavish amenities such as leather club chairs and antique billiard tables. In addition, men were treated to therapeutic massages at the twice-monthly men's smokers.

Executive offices for the club manager and staff were small and were located in the basement of the building away from operations. Other space in the clubhouse included the Great Lounge near the front door, golf and tennis pro shops, storage rooms, and employee facilities.

The caddie shack was located next to the men's locker room. The caddie staff, each considered an independent contractor, used the men's locker room toilet facilities and showers. Caddies were required to report each day at 6:00 a.m. to the caddie master and pay the club a $20 per day "caddie privilege fee" for the ability to hire out to members. The club instituted this policy as an income producer to make up for lost cart revenue. Except for the daily fee, caddies were allowed to keep their earnings and tips.

Pro Shops

The golf pro shop was located at the north end of the building with no view of either starting hole, the cart staging area, or the caddie shack. The club owned the golf pro shop operation. Including clothing and equipment, the average monthly inventory ran $200,000 on retail sales of $50,000. Cost of sales averaged 75 percent.

The tennis pro shop was located next to the golf pro shop with no view of the courts or pool (the director of tennis was also in charge of the pool operation). The club owned the tennis pro shop operation. Including clothing and equipment, the average monthly inventory ran $15,000 on retail sales of $2,500. Cost of sales averaged 80%. Tennis members generally frequented the discount houses for clothing and equipment. According to the director of tennis, "The cheap jerks will cut your throat for a dollar."

The Club discontinued food and beverage at the courtside pavilion since the manager felt the low volume did not warrant the service. As a response, the director of tennis began personally buying beer at the grocery store and sold iced-down single cans in a makeshift concession. The manager said, "Just don't tell me about it."

The Golf Courses

The newer eighteen holes of the club only slightly resembled the older course. Both golf courses were designed by members of the Jones family. While the design was excellent, a number of shortcuts were taken in the construction of the North Course. For example, greens drainage is inadequate during the monsoon season, leaving standing water on the greens for up to twenty-four hours at a time. Bunkers were not properly constructed with internal drains, creating similar standing water problems and inconsistent sand conditions. Finally, the parallel irrigation system was stretched from 35-foot (recommended spacing) to 45-foot head spacing to save approximately $20,000 in construction costs. Jones was furious. During the summer, the course browns out in high spots and becomes soggy in low spots.

Generally, the older members prefer the South Course for its scenic beauty and because its shorter distance allows them a better opportunity to score well. Younger members lean toward the North Course for its macho image and challenge. On Wednesday afternoons, the North Course draws a notorious crowd of approximately six foursomes that call themselves the Gunslingers. It is rumored they play for high stakes—as much as $1,000 per round; settle up in the men's card room after playing. Because of the high pressure and high stakes, settling up is usually accompanied by filthy language and abusive outbursts directed toward the female staff. Despite the hostile atmosphere, it is estimated that approximately half of the female staff serving in the men's card room date the male members. This interaction creates problems in scheduling for the food and beverage manager when a date goes sour. Most of the female staff in the men's card room are from Asian countries and speak English as a second language.

The greens on the North Course have experienced a natural transition over the years. The grass composition is approximately half Bentgrass (Penncross) and half Poa Annua, which creates an uneven putting surface. The club is considering re-grassing the North greens by one of two methods: grow-in the greens from seed (SR1020) nine holes at a time or grow sod on vacant land elsewhere on the property, harvest it, and lay it in one hole at a time. The South greens are 100 percent SR1020 Bentgrass—firm and true. The fairways replenish themselves rapidly (328 and 419 Bermuda), and the tee boxes (same as fairway grasses) are ample and configured into banana shapes to allow several different locations for each tee, thereby reducing the probability of wearing out any single tee spots. The rough grass is common Bermuda.

Golf Course Maintenance

Only three individuals have held the position of golf course superintendent. The most recent superintendent, Jimbo, has been in the business over 40 years, hates his mostly Hispanic staff, and hates the members even more. He came to the club in 1985 and is known for running his own show. Although he technically reports to the general manager, the general manager allows Jimbo the freedom to free-wheel as long as he gets the job done. Course conditioning is good. Overall, the members are quite pleased. Jimbo does not attend greens committee meetings since he thinks that members only know enough about grass to get into trouble. He has run an informal business out of the golf maintenance area for the past ten years. In Jimbo's sideline business, outside of his duties as golf course superintendent, he allows his workers to cut homeowners' grass using club equipment. He justifies the business by saying it allows his guys to make a few extra bucks. The general manager quietly allows this arrangement for the good of the workers.

Outbuildings

Equipment and cart storage buildings were built along with the clubhouse in 1973. A recent housing development complains about early-morning noise of equipment used to get the course ready for play. Some of the residents have threatened to sue the club if it does not agree to delay cutting the greens until after 8:00 a.m.

The original buildings were not adequate to house the equipment for the South Course. The golf course superintendent supervised the construction of two additional buildings. Connections in the industry allowed him to save significantly on building costs for the club. In doing so, however, he never obtained permits for the buildings and underground storage tanks for diesel and gasoline. In addition, the wash-down operation drains directly into the canyon stream that eventually runs into the ocean near Laguna Beach.

One issue facing the club board today is how to replace the existing concrete-shingled roof on the principal equipment building. In recent years, the roof has shown signs of significant wear from golf balls from the practice range hitting it, and it is leaking. The club has two bids for repair. The lower one is for $77,500 to replace the roof on the principal equipment building. The golf course superintendent says he can arrange to have it taken care of for $25,000 if he does not have to use a licensed roofer.

Town of Tarantula Canyon, California

The town of Tarantula Canyon (population 4,000) lies east of the club property boundary across Old Hogback Road. Tarantula Canyon was founded in the early 1900s as an outpost community for ranchers, farmers, and equestrian enthusiasts. The expansive grasslands near Tarantula Canyon had been farmed and grazed for years before the club's founding in 1973. Today, Tarantula Canyon is primarily a farming community. Barley is the principal cash crop, although several large orna-mental horticulture companies remain in operation in the area as well. On the south end of the club property, a nominal lease exists over two thousand acres of future development area for a cattle rancher to graze beef cattle. The published benefit to the developer is that grazing keeps the dry grasslands from creating a fire hazard for the surrounding homeowners in the canyon. The developer does not discuss an underlying benefit—that the cattle trample a potential nesting habitat of the Blue Thrush Whippie, an endangered species bird in the State of California. Discovery of habitat for an endangered species severely limits development. State law provides that upon discovery of habitat for an endangered species, a buffer zone is automatically created that runs 1,000 feet out from the perimeter of the habitat, which is then declared off limits for any type of development. While Tarantula Canyon enjoyed prosperity during the early farming and ranching years, it has been a relatively depressed area since the early 1950s. Generally, the town has always supported the club because of the infusion of jobs and cash it has pro-vided for the community. A total of fifty Tarantula Canyon locals work at the club.

High-end, multi-acreage, single-family residential development has made it as far south as Tarantula Canyon. However, production housing—considered more affordable—still remains approximately ten miles to the north. Many of the members live about twenty miles north of the club in Cricket Junction, a commu-nity that has enjoyed relatively stable growth throughout the last two decades. Some members blame the Tarantula Canyon council for the lack of residential tracts in the area due to a long-standing ordinance that allows for tax-free farming and other agriculture, and the stand taken against development by those who believe that such developments would unfairly compete for the limited water sup-ply. Member attitudes are mixed: some want to live closer to the club; others want to preserve the rural atmosphere. The developer of the club wants to begin devel-oping tract homes along the golf course. He believes the time is right to cash in on the population movement to the south from Los Angeles.

A substantial internship program, initiated at the club to allow college stu-dents from Cal Poly to work at the club part time, has caused relationships with club employees to become strained over the last decade. Old-timers feel the col-lege students are competing for their jobs and object to the students' push for par-ticipatory management and more say about workplace policy. In addition, there is resentment toward the Asian women who work in the men's grill and card room area; they seem to be exempted from following any rules at all.

The club's relationship with Tarantula Canyon has also become strained over the part-time status of the club's employees. When the club transitioned from essentially full-time workers to a small core of full-timers supported by many part-time and on-call positions, the unemployment rate in Tarantula Canyon went up to more than 20 percent. The club's attorney has also advised the manager and board that if the club makes it a point to employ Tarantula Canyon locals for less than four months, it is not necessary to follow many state and federal employment laws and guidelines. This mean that the club can save substantially on health, workers' compensation, and retirement benefits by employing workers for less than twenty-six consecutive weeks, and, if it follows this policy, the club also will not be subject to many standard discrimination laws—for example, the Americans with Disabilities Act, the Pregnancy Discrimination Act, and the Vietnam Veterans Act. The club has followed this policy vigorously in recent years and has successfully reduced its benefits costs from 30 percent to 17 percent of gross payroll. Some employees have discussed this situation with representatives of a local union.

Bad blood exists over this issue between many Tarantula Canyon locals and the club. According to the manager, while the club has been successful in some ways, such as in reducing costs, it may have lost in other ways. Many club employees appear to perform at levels that are well below the performance levels that existed before the new cut and slash policy was initiated. Examples of such poor performance include a decline in service, employee tardiness, and absenteeism rates higher than those previously experienced. A widely held rumor around the club is that some employees have, on occasion, also sabotaged food orders in various ways. Warm, friendly smiles have been replaced by depersonalization and frowns—that is, surly service. Members complain that they are no longer made to feel special and have circulated several petitions expressing their dissatisfaction.

Club Facing a New Competitor

Membership at Blue Thistle Country Club has remained fairly stable. However, now the club faces the proposed development of a new private club in Tarantula Canyon. Land has already been purchased, and groundbreaking for the high-end Palmer eighteen-hole golf course is scheduled for spring. According to reliable sources, the new club will target golfers rather than country clubbers and will have an initiation fee of $90,000. Dues at the new club will be $900 per month including carts, lockers, bags, and shoe service. There will be no food and beverage minimum. According to sources, the proposed memberships will be sold as equity certificates and can be sold upon resignation for market rate less a club transfer fee of $20,000.

Included in the organizing group of the new club are several current Blue Thistle Country Club members. Rumor has it that the proposed club has already signed up 100 members. Those interested in membership believe they are better off owning their club as equity members rather than participating in a developer-owned club. They also feel they can offer greater exclusivity by being more selective in choosing members.

Plans for the new club include a more conventional returning-nine type golf course, traditional clubhouse, modern exercise facility, indoor pool and Jacuzzi, and casual and formal dining facilities. The Blue Thistle manager has learned that the new club will not allow outside functions. In addition, the new club will be chartered as a not-for-profit, tax-exempt entity.

Events Involving the Club

Blue Thistle Country Club has been forced to address other issues of significant importance. First, the club has been named in a discrimination suit filed regarding its tee time policies. The rule at Blue Thistle Country Club is that tee times from 8:00 to 11:00 a.m. during the week and 7:00 a.m. to noon on Saturday are reserved for men only. The suit charges that this policy is discriminatory. The suit was filed by a female member of the club who is known for taking strong stands on issues she believes in. She is a senior partner in a large Los Angeles law firm specializing in discrimination suits.

The second issue is an accident that occurred last year. A mower being operated on the fairway in a proper manner ran over a rock, which was thrown by the blades approximately 100 feet, striking a guest in the face. The guest lost sight in his left eye. He has sued the club for negligence as well as emergency care, physician and hospital care, and extensive medical rehabilitation. He tried unsuccessfully to work with the club's insurance company, claiming he only wanted them to respond to him as a person. In other words, he says he really did not want to sue, but the insurance company made him very angry in its no-response handling of the incident.

The third situation involves a former bartender. An evening manager witnessed a bartender drinking behind the bar and slurring his words. When the bartender went on break, the manager smelled the glass and discovered that it contained liquor. The bartender came back while the manager was still examining the glass. The manager told the bartender to clock out and that there would be an investigation. He then asked the night guard to drive the bartender home. A struggle ensued between the night guard and the bartender in the parking lot, and the bartender jumped into his car and drove away. On his way home, he was involved in an accident and was killed. The bartender's family has sued the club for permitting a known alcoholic to drink on the job and to drive home. The manager was aware that the bartender had a drinking problem.

The final issue threatening the club concerns the dismissal of a female captain who worked in the men's card room. The captain, Phan Quen, a Tarantula Canyon resident of Asian descent, was arrested. She was allegedly engaging in activities associated with possession with intent to distribute cocaine and involvement with ongoing prostitution. The arrest was widely reported in the newspaper. The club manager appealed to the board for advice regarding this issue. On their unofficial advice, the manager fired the employee to minimize bad publicity. During the investigation, the employee was found innocent on the cocaine matter, and she is suing the club for punitive damages regarding her dismissal and for slander. The board is concerned since it has become common knowledge that several male members of the club are involved with her as prostitution customers.

The manager says he has tapes of the prostitution incidents recorded by secret cameras he had installed throughout the club last year after he heard such activities were occurring on club property. He feels he has airtight evidence on that matter. However, he says he may have acted too quickly on the alleged cocaine incident. In his story, the manager said he had searched Phan's employee locker and found a sandwich bag containing approximately two ounces of what appeared to be cocaine. He turned it over to the police, who later determined that the bag contained an exotic type of borax powder (used to crisp-up wonton wrappers) from Asia that the chef had asked Phan to pick up in Little Saigon, an area near Los Angeles. She had simply stored the bag in her locker until the chef returned from vacation.

Many female club employees working in the men's grill have sided with Phan. They have become outraged that the male members of the club continue to berate them with abusive outbursts and filthy language in the card room. One female employee has suggested to other employees that they could each file charges of sexual harassment with the Equal Employment Opportunity Commission (EEOC) because of this hostile treatment. It is rumored certain employees have had conversations with the female member who works for the law firm specializing in discrimination suits.

Revenues

In 1973, the club opened with 100 golf members, and it grew to its initial cap of 500 golf members by 1995. With the addition of the South Course, memberships were again opened, and today the club has 1,000 golf members. Another 250 members hold tennis memberships (there are nine courts), and there are an additional 500 social members. Tennis and social members are allowed to play golf once per quarter by paying a guest-of-golf-member greens fee.

Since the property is still being developed and is controlled by the developer—a partnership comprised of the original developer-investors and Canyon Oil—all memberships are nonequity. Initiation fees at the club are currently $80,000 for golf, $2,000 for tennis, and $1,500 for social membership. Members receive a 75 percent refund of their initiation fee deposit on a one-for-one basis upon resignation. Monthly fees are $700 per month for golf, $250 for tennis, and $100 for social. Members are also assessed an additional food and beverage minimum of $100 per quarter. The club is debt free and has been cash flow positive since 2000.

In 2003, the Club recorded positive cash flow of $4,000,000 including spending $800,000 in capital expenditures to cover replacement of worn-out equipment.

However, trends since 2000 have created little to no growth in food and beverage sales. While more covers are being served, member preferences have turned toward value pricing and more casual, moderately priced selections. The food and beverage department has countered this trend by eliminating free morning coffee, raising prices moderately, cutting down on portion sizes, and purchasing cheaper well brands instead of using a premium well as had been the practice. These actions have disturbed several members and have resulted in a boycott of the dining room. The old-time regulars are grousing about changes and want a return to previous food and beverage policies.

While sales have declined, costs continue to rise. One manager has suggested that profits are walking out the back door in the arms of employees who regularly take both food and money from the club. The general manager is sympathetic toward the old-guard employees and has allowed them to eat mistakes and take home leftovers. He does not seem concerned that a great deal of theft may be occurring. He admits that there is a trusting atmosphere in the club and the employees do have opportunities to take advantage if they so desire.

One member who works for a computer company says that the club could buy a new computerized point-of-sale (POS) system that rings up food and beverage sales, tracks tee times and reservations, and computes payroll. They could pay for the system just from the savings of stolen and wasted inventory. He has offered his services to the club in developing a proposal to eliminate each of these problems.

Members of the social committee believe that food sales are dependent on the success of major functions in the club and that the quality of these functions has been poor. Examples used by these members include the food at the Member-Guest Tournament, the Fall Classic, the Member-Member Tournament, and the annual Spring Stampede. Records indicate that attendance at these events is down.

Upcoming events are promoted through a monthly calendar mailed to members' addresses on the 27th of each month. Similarly, events are reinforced in a mailing on the 12th of the month. Posters are hung throughout the club for major events, and placemat reminders are copied and used in the grill to encourage members to sign up. Members still say they do not know what is happening with regard to upcoming functions at the club.

Questions

Identify and rate problems by degree:
1. Identify a minimum of five *critical* issues requiring immediate attention (numbered A1-A5).
2. Identify five *necessary* issues (not critical) to address within six months (numbered B1-B5).
3. Identify five *important* issues (important, but not necessary) which should be adopted into the Club philosophy over a period of time (numbered C1–C5).

Work Morale and Motivation

Objectives

At the completion of the case study, students should be able to:

1. Describe the function of human resource management in a hospitality context.
2. Explain the legal aspects of human resource management within the hospitality industry.
3. Evaluate employee benefit administration, employee rights, and labor relations.

Case Study Narrative

A private membership country club in the Midwest faced a serious decline in employee morale and motivation, which resulted in management confrontation within the organization. The employees have been complaining about not receiving any pay raises within the past two years. The organization used the excuse that the company has been struggling financially. The employees are not aware of such serious financial problems and believe that leadership and management style are the root causes. The employees believe that the top management does not appreciate the hard work that everyone contributes to the organization. The employees intend to leave the organization as a consequence of the perceived unfair labor practices. Even though the employee turnover rate is high and is one of the most serious problems in the hospitality industry, this country club is not treating its employees fairly because the organization thinks that hospitality laborers are not highly skilled or educated and can be replaced by anyone at any time. The employees also believe that managers are paid too much in terms of their contributions to the organization's effectiveness.

The worst business practice is that management asks most of the kitchen staff and restaurant servers to come in one hour early and leave one hour late without any extra hourly compensation. The management is trying to save on labor costs by making its employees work extra hours without pay. The manager told the employees, for example, to come in at 7:00 A.M., but not to clock in until 8:00 A.M.; therefore depriving the employees of one additional hour of pay. This practice further convinces the employees that the management is taking advantage of them. Since they are supposedly not highly trained or educated, the management feels that the employees cannot understand how their rights are being violated and they will compromise in order to keep their jobs. The employees are always discussing this problem among themselves, but are not willing to share their grievances with the managers.

In the past, the country club had a salary and bonus incentive program that rightly compensated the employees for their work efforts. The organization cancelled most of these, along with other incentive programs, disappointing the employees even more. The result is that employees are not motivated to do their personal best in exerting high effort in their work. There is talk among the employees about quitting their jobs because of the disrespect from the management and the unethical management practices and lack of pay incentives.

Questions

1. What did the management do wrong in this case?
2. What can the management do to improve the current situation?
3. What can the employees do to better protect their rights?
4. How can the stereotyping of hospitality employees (low skills and education required) be changed?
5. What can be done to reduce the high employee turnover rate in the hospitality industry?

Cases in Tourism

THE ADIRONDACKS: HUMAN AND NATURE TOURISM PARTNERSHIP

DEVELOPING JORDANIAN TOURISM PRODUCTS AND SERVICES

MOUNT EVANS SCENIC BYWAY: IS IT BEING LOVED TO DEATH? OR IS THIS A BUSINESS OPPORTUNITY?

BORDER TOURISM SYNERGIES IN THE NORTH COUNTRY: NEW YORK AND QUEBEC

The Adirondacks

Human and Nature Tourism Partnership

Objectives

At the completion of this case study, students should be able to:

1. Assess a natural attraction.
2. Understand the nature of public and private partnerships.
3. Research unique natural areas.
4. Understand preservation and ethics in the environment.

Case Study Narrative

The Adirondacks have long been known for outdoor recreation activities. Hiking, biking, fishing, and wildlife viewing (birds, moose, bears, or deer) are common pursuits for visitors. The Adirondack Park is 5.8 million acres including 12 counties and 92 towns (Higgins and Holmes 1999). Abundant in natural resources and open space, the Adirondack Park is unique to New York and the United States. The wild forest, water, wildlife, aesthetic resources of the park, and its open space character provide outdoor recreational experiences of national and international significance. The park is central to the economic base of the local tourism industry and constitutes a resource, an opportunity, and a constraint (Draper and Driscoll 1991). A growing population, advancing technology, and an expanding economy focus ever-increasing pressures on these priceless resources (APAA 1998).

The Adirondacks are a prime example of a recreational area that requires management by sustainable tourism standards. Responsible tourism for park lands needs planning and marketing that can provide tourists with meaningful visits, allow businesses in the local area to benefit, ensure the integrity of the destination, and develop a positive relationship between the local population and the destination managers (United States Forest Service 1993). The Adirondacks offer a unique park environment that includes sites such as Lake Placid, which has resorts, restaurants, and Olympic venues.

Lake Placid, and other host communities in the Adirondacks, must balance the need for visitors with the social, cultural, physical, economic, psychological, and environmental impacts on the community.

The use of the Adirondacks depends on responsible actions toward the natural environment there. The real issue is how to convey this environmental ethics message to the adults who are the real users of the resource. Hiking permits and penalties for abuse are possibilities, but the cost of enforcement is too great to make this system work throughout the vast park. Each human institution (e.g., resorts, restaurants) in the park and local community must interact, taking into consideration the economic, environmental, social, cultural, psychological, and physical impacts each could have on the other.

Thinking About the Future

A study by Higgins and Holmes (1999) on the Adirondacks and its relationship to tourism and business in general identified several themes. These themes include:

- Little reliable data on tourism demand.
- Lack of regional and local planning.
- Effectiveness of tourism marketing strategies virtually unknown.
- Economic, social, and environmental impacts of tourism on local communities and the region as a whole seldom identified.

The following questions reflect other information needed to make better decisions about tourism:

- Who are our visitors?
- Where did they hear about us?
- What is the level of visitor satisfaction?
- What do visitors wish was here?
- What are they looking for?
- What do they think of when they think of the Adirondacks?
- What would entice them?
- Where else are they going on vacation?

Perhaps the most important question is what is the appropriate level of visitation to promote sustainability? The Adirondack Park Plan already includes much of the needed documentation for appropriate levels of park use.

In the past, the intermingling of public and private land enhanced the Adirondack environment. This fruitful relationship is now jeopardized by the threat of unregulated development on such private lands. Local governments in the Adirondack Park find it increasingly difficult to cope with unrelenting pressures for development being brought to the area. The basic purpose of this act is to ensure optimum overall conservation, protection, preservation, development, and use of unique scenic, aesthetic, wildlife, recreational, open space, historic, and ecological and natural resources of the Adirondack Park (APAA). Critical issues to be examined are:

- The number of visitors the park can support (carrying capacity).
- Partnerships between the Adirondack Park; the City of Plattsburgh, New York; and the State University of New York (SUNY), Plattsburgh.
- Interpretation and information distribution.

Two decades ago, Reime and Hawkins (1980) discussed the task of matching future tourism developments with homogeneous markets and the analysis of the following:

- What are the natural, social, and cultural characteristics where the development is to occur?
- What are the characteristics and needs of the various segments of the tourism market?
- What additional infrastructure is required to satisfy the needs of a particular market segment?

Using these questions as a benchmark, the need for the Adirondack Park administrators to develop and implement a system of sustainable management is critical. The Adirondack Park is the key tourism attraction in the North Country. However, from the gateway areas to the park, what, if any, information is readily available? In a previous study, Gunn (1994) pointed out that the area needs to attract environmentally appropriate industries and expand tourism. Regional tourism planning indicates that the following three park-wide concepts are essential:

1. Develop a regional network of tourist information and interpretative centers.
2. Identify amenity areas and recreation zones.
3. Identify recreation and tourism routes.

According to Gunn (1994), there should be a major regional facility near the center of the park, and this center should be complemented by eight to ten gateway facilities in strategic communities. This network of centers would add greatly to the understanding and appreciation of the Adirondack Park.

The Adirondack Park, as a tourism attraction that rivals many of the national parks, provides the North Country of New York with a unique opportunity to enhance commercial tourism while developing and managing that tourism in a sustainable manner. Working toward these goals will produce positive results for the Adirondack Park; SUNY–Plattsburgh; and the City of Plattsburgh. The City of Plattsburgh and SUNY–Plattsburgh are strategically located to the northeast of the park and can use their location to promote the community and to involve the park and its resources in the college's programs. Creating the synergies needed to benefit the region is the next step toward developing sustainable tourism in this beautiful region.

Questions

1. What are some tactics and strategies that need to be used to make this a workable situation for the environment and private enterprise?
2. Who might the partners be in this type of situation?
3. How will the message of environmental ethics be promoted?
4. Where will the information distribution centers be established?

References

Adirondack Park Act 1 (APAA) 1998, Section 802, State of New York, Albany, New York.

Draper, D., and A. Driscoll. 1991. *Development dilemmas: Enhancing sustainable tourism through cooperative choices; Quality tourism—Concept of a sustainable tourism development, harmonizing economical, social and ecological interests,* Reports presented at the 41st Congress de FAIEST, November 17–23, Seychelles. pp. 23, 157–183.

Gunn, C. 1994. *Tourism planning: Basics, concepts, cases.* Philadelphia: Taylor & Francis.

Hawley, A. H. 1973. Human Ecology. In M. Micklin (ed.), *Population, environment and social organization.* New York: Taylor & Francis, pp. 27–42.

Higgins, B., and T. Holmes. 1999. *Tourism business, community and the environment in the Adirondack Park: The perspectives of business owners and managers in the central and western Adirondack Park.* Bronx, N.Y.: Wildlife Conservation Society.

Reime, M., and C. Hawkins. 1980. Planning and Developing Hospitality Facilities that Increase Tourist Demand. In D. Hawkins, E. L. Shafer, and J. M. Rovelstad. (eds.), *Tourism marketing and management issues.* Washington, D.C.: George Washington University, pp. 239–248.

United States Forest Service. 1993. *Guiding principles,* Lakewood, Colo.: USFS Regional Office.

Developing Jordanian Tourism Products and Services

Objectives

At the completion of this case study, students should be able to:

1. Assess tourism products in Jordan and other locations.
2. Propose a sustainable tourism plan.

Case Study Narrative

The Hashemite Kingdom of Jordan

Officials at the Jordan Ministry of Tourism contemplated the development of their tourism industry and the tourism product. As a group, they felt the country had great potential for tourism and this development would be a boon to the economy. Despite the troubled past of the region, Jordan has historically been a stable environment. Their first step was to assess the attractions and infrastructure of the country.

Arab hospitality is evidenced when a visitor to Jordan is greeted by "Ahlan wa sahlan," which means welcome. Jordan is positioned at the core of the Middle East, and it has been a stabilizing force in this region. Situated as it is between the great civilizations of Egypt to the west and Mesopotamia to the east, Jordan was destined to be a busy crossroads (Ministry of Tourism and Antiquities 1997). Above all, Jordan is a land of history, and new details of its ancient civilizations are coming to light every year, as archeological teams probe into the Jordanian earth in search of the past (Ministry of Tourism and Antiquities 1997). The country of Jordan covers an area of 96,188 square kilometers. Syria borders it on the north, Iraq and Saudi Arabia on the east, Saudi Arabia on the south, and the occupied West Bank on the west (Ministry of Tourism and Antiquities 1997). The country boasts one of the world's most pleasant climates and is often compared to southern California.

99

Jordan has an estimated population of 4 million people and has a constitutional monarchy form of government (Ministry of Tourism and Antiquities 1997).

Jordanian Tourism

In the *Jordan Tourism Cluster Report* (Hashemite Kingdom of Jordan 1996), it was noted that visitors to Jordan stay for an average of four days. This is low compared to regional competitors such as Egypt, with a stay of 8 days, and Israel, with a stay of 18 days. In addition, tourists spend significantly less per visit in Jordan than in its regional competitors. If the Jordanian tourism industry were able to get every tourist to spend one more day in the country, it would increase the total tourism receipts by 25 percent.

Currently the mix of visitors to Jordan by geographic origin is Arab countries 52 percent, Israel 11 percent, Europe 23 percent, North and South America 10 percent, and others 4 percent. The major reasons for visiting Jordan have been identified as follows:

- To visit relatives
- For trading and investment
- To attend conferences and workshops
- For sporting events
- For entertainment
- For medical services
- For its culture
- To see its holy sites
- To view its historical sites

The Ministry of Tourism also identifies what it refers to as a *hidden segment*. This segment of visitors is from the Gulf countries and is predominantly made up of families who often spend the entire summer in furnished apartments in Jordan, attracted by the entertainment options available there (Hashemite Kingdom of Jordan 1996).

In a comparison of tourism revenues from Jordan with its neighboring competitors, Jordan lags behind, as shown in Table 1.

Jordanian Tourism Experienced.   This illustrates a proposed standard for Jordanian tourism and the details a sampling of the tourism product and services in Jordan.

Table 1   Industry Performance Indicators

	Jordan	Egypt	Israel
Number of tourists (thousands)	1103	3675	2097
Revenues (US$ millions)	770	3200	2800
Revenue per tourist (US$)	698	871	1335

World Tourism Organization, Middle East 1997, 1996.

The theme(s) for tourism in the Hashemite Kingdom of Jordan are Legend, History, and Hospitality (Ministry of Tourism and Antiquities 1998). The hypothesis is that by focusing on tourism industry issues—such as people, attractions, activities, and infrastructure—Jordan can achieve a balance of livability, visitation, and sustainability.

Jordan also has an opportunity to enhance its tourism product through various other themes of tourism. Cultural tourism can focus on the people of Jordan, one of the country's strongest assets. Jordan's people are friendly and welcoming, and visitors will want to know about traditions and ethnic groups, such as the Bedouins and others. Cultural tourism could also include food. In addition, the emphasis on crafts appears to be rising, and a tie with Queen Noor's foundation and other crafts projects would enhance the cultural attraction.

Segments of Tourism. Specific segments and attractions need to be considered in the development of tourism in Jordan. The following highlights some of these;

Accommodations

Natural Attractions
- Dead Sea
- Dana Wildlife Reserve (DWR)
- Wadi Rum

Cultural Attractions
- Madaba
- Mt. Nebo
- Petra
- Aljoun Castle
- Um Qais
- Desert Castles Route

Tourism Infrastructure Issues
- Waste management
- Highways and scenic byways
- Signage
- Shopping

Health Tourism
- Hot springs and spas

Special Events
- Festivals
- Concerts

Ingress and Egress to and from Jordan

Tourism's Future in Jordan

Jordan has some of the most outstanding sites of any country in the world. Petra, in particular, and the general cultural and natural environment of the country offer interesting tourism opportunities. The overall level of development that exists for tourism products and services is generally low, but this can be used to advantage in creating a sustainable development mode that will ensure a strong tourism product for years to come.

In short, Jordan has a chance to do it correctly. So often tourism development is handled badly through poor planning and haste to make profit. Jordan is not an inexpensive tourist destination, and therefore the opportunity to provide a value-added, cutting-edge, sustainable development product is necessary to position Jordanian tourism in the future. Developing resources in a sustainable way means managing resources in such a way as to fulfill economic, social, and aesthetic needs while maintaining cultural integrity, essential ecological processes, biological diversity, and life support systems (Tourism Canada 1990).

Decision-Making Data

Developing practical and scientifically sound approaches to constructing and reporting indices related to recreation and tourism trends is necessary for planning and management functions, as well as for other purposes such as accountability and educational materials (Dawson 1985). A useful strategy would be the formation of alliances with Jordanian universities to conduct ongoing tourism data research and testing.

Jordan's information channels appear unstructured between organizations and institutions that have not traditionally been considered interconnected. The goal could be for Jordan to act as a united tourism entity with all aspects linked. Clearly, the level of sophistication for the business and government decision makers needs to include awareness or an awakening of the interrelationship between tourism and a cross-section of Jordanian issues such as adequate transportation, education, and human resources, as well as other infrastructure development.

Interpretation

In addition to further tour guide training, there is work to be done in the area of interpretation. The brochures produced by the Ministry of Tourism and Antiquities are beautiful and informative. However, more in-depth materials could be available at individual sites. In addition, more interpretative displays and signage would enhance visitors' experiences throughout the country. Tour guides in Jordan vary in their expertise and quality. In Jerash, researchers participated in one of the best-guided experiences one could have. In Petra, while the tour guide was a very welcoming individual, there was much more that could have been done with guide training to enhance the visit. One idea is to use students as interns or employees to better complement the guide workforce.

Conclusion

Overall, Jordan has a high-quality tourism product, but pieces of the infrastructure need review, evaluation, and polish. Jordanian tourism is positioned to capitalize on its strengths. Tourism, when developed correctly and thoughtfully with full participation by all segments of the industry, can provide many positive benefits for both visitors and the people and land of Jordan.

Questions

1. How should Jordan tourism products be packaged?
2. How does Jordan's location in the middle of world events and fighting impact its tourism product?
3. How will the issue of enhanced tourism be promoted to the local population as well as to potential tourists?
4. How will infrastructure issues be addressed (waste, water, security, transportation) to make a trip to Jordan achievable?

References

Dawson, C. P. 1985. Monitoring Local Trends in Recreation and Tourism Through Visitor Statistical Abstracts. In James D. Woods, Jr. (ed.), *Proceedings.* 1985 Natural Outdoor Recreation Trends Symposium II. National Park Service, U.S. Department of Interior.

Hashemite Kingdom of Jordan. 1996. *The Tourism Cluster Report.* Kingdom of Jordan.

Ministry of Tourism and Antiquities. 1997. *Jordan where adventure awaits you: Faces and places in time,* Amman: Jordan Tourism Board.

Ministry of Tourism and Antiquities. 1998. *Hashemite Kingdom of Jordan: The Tourism Cluster.* Hashemite Kingdom of Jordan.Tourism Canada. 1990. http://www.canadatourism.com/ctx/app/en/ca/home.do Accessed 1997.

Tourism Canada. 1990. http://www.canadatourism.com/ctx/app/en/ca/home.do Accessed 1997.

Mount Evans Scenic Byway

Is It Being Loved to Death?
Or Is This a Business Opportunity?

Objectives

At the completion of this case study, students should be able to:

1. Analyze a natural area for sustainable development action plans.
2. Identify partners for business success.
3. Generate operating alternatives for natural areas.
4. Describe existing business models in natural areas.

Case Study Narrative

Mount Evans has long been known for recreation and activities. Hiking, biking, fishing, wildlife viewing (mountain goat herds), and picnicking are commons pursuits for visitors. Summit Lake, a common stop for most visitors, was designated a Natural History Landmark in 1965. Mount Evans Wilderness Area, located on the Mount Evans Scenic Byway, contains many of the oldest known bristlecone pines in the country and possesses a unique ecology that attracts researchers and scientists from around the country. Mount Evans is a prime example of a recreational site that requires management by ecotourism standards. Responsible tourism development for the Byway will demonstrate the need for planning and marketing that can provide tourists with meaningful visits, allow businesses in the local area to benefit, ensure the integrity of the destination, and develop a positive relationship between the local population and the destination managers (United States Forest Service 1993).

An interagency task force was appointed to work on developing a plan for the Mount Evans Corridor and ultimately the Mount Evans Scenic Byway. Once a plan was developed, the team's charge was to report back to its respective agencies and organizations. Integrating the interagency issues that are involved and the input from the general public make this a difficult assignment. The United States Forest Service (USFS) plays a major role in this project because the area is surrounded by the Arapaho/Roosevelt National Forest. While the USFS is not in charge of the partnership, USFS representatives have acted as a catalyst for the group. USFS guiding principles frame the approach taken to work on the Mount Evans plan (Figure 1).

In addition, the USFS mission is exemplified in the motto "Caring for Land and Serving the People." The motto mirrors the Mount Evans Planning Team concerns and advocates certain precepts of Mount Evans planning and management (Figure 2).

These precepts emphasize involvement and potential partnerships for the Byway effort. They are much more than phrases, reflecting a frame of mind for responsible tourism development and management.

The Planning Effort

The purpose of this planning effort is to provide a management framework designed to coordinate agency activities, improve customer service, improve resource protection and management, and develop partnership opportunities (Wong 1993). From

---

- Use an ecological approach to the multiple use management of the National Forests and Grasslands.
- Use the best scientific knowledge in making decisions and select the most appropriate technologies in the management of resources.
- Be good neighbors who respect private property rights.
- Strive for quality and excellence in everything we do and be sensitive to the effects of our decisions on people and resources.
- Strive to meet the needs of our customers in fair, friendly, and open ways. Form partnerships to achieve shared goals.
- Promote grass-roots participation in our decisions and activities. Value and trust one another and share leadership.
- Value a multicultural organization as essential to our success. Maintain high professional and ethical standards. Be responsible and accountable for what is done. Recognize and accept that some conflict is natural and strive to deal with it professionally.
- Follow laws, regulations, executive direction, and congressional intent.

Source: USFS 1993.

Figure 1   USFS Guiding Principles

- Advocating a conservation ethic in promoting the health, productivity, diversity, and beauty of forests and associated lands.
- Listening to people and responding to their diverse needs in making decisions.
- Protecting and managing resources so they best demonstrate the sustainable use management concept.
- Providing technical and financial assistance to state and private forest landowners, encouraging them to practice good stewardship and quality land management in meeting their specific objectives.
- Providing technical and financial assistance to cities and communities to improve their natural environment by planting trees and caring for their forests.
- Providing international technical assistance and scientific exchanges to sustain and enhance global resources and to encourage quality land management.
- Helping partners to wisely use the forests to promote rural economic development and a quality rural environment.
- Developing and providing scientific and technical knowledge aimed at improving our capability to protect, manage, and use natural resources.
- Providing work, training, and education to the unemployed, underemployed, elderly, youth, and disadvantaged in pursuit of our mission.

Source: USFS 1993.

Figure 2   Caring for the Land and Serving People

a Forest Service perspective, the key questions to be addressed in this planning process are:

1. Who will manage the Byway?
2. Who will maintain existing facilities?
3. Should private vehicles continue to be allowed to drive to the top of the mountain?
4. Can fees be charged to those driving to the top?
5. What is the optimal carrying capacity for the Mount Evans Corridor?
6. Should a private concession operator run buses to the top for fees?
7. How will any initiative(s) be funded? (Wong 1993).

To answer these questions, decision makers have to consider the true significance of Mount Evans and its environment. The Forest Service's statement of significance illustrates its importance (Figure 3).

1. Mount Evans Corridor is the highest paved auto road in North America, climbing to 14,264 feet above sea level.
2. The Summit Lake area was the first designated Natural History Landmark in North America.
3. The University of Denver Observatory at the summit of Mount Evans is the highest observatory in the world.
4. Mount Evans was the first road in Colorado designed specifically for its scenic beauty.
5. The Mount Evans Wilderness Area is bounded by the Mount Evans Corridor on both sides.
6. Mount Evans is a major tourism destination for Colorado, drawing local and international visitors for the many recreational opportunities offered at this diverse area (bikers, hikers, photographers, hunters, nature watchers, writers, researchers, motorcyclists, anglers, educators, and botanists).
7. Mount Evans is readily accessible to the 2.0 million people residing in Denver and its many suburbs.
8. Mount Evans offers unique wildlife viewing opportunities including the most accessible Rocky Mountain goat herd in Colorado, if not the entire United States.
9. The Mount Evans area contains many of the oldest known bristlecone pines in Colorado.
10. The Mount Evans area offers unique interpretation and research opportunities because of the dramatic life zone transitions and the accessibility of the areas to be studied.
11. It is one of the few areas in the United States that has true permafrost.
12. The unique ecology of Mount Evans attracts researchers and scientists from around the world.
13. Visitors are able to experience the transition between the three life zones of Mount Evans, one would need to travel 3,000 miles north to the Arctic Circle to have a similar experience.

Source: USFS 1993.

Figure 3   Statement of Significance

Additional questions include those of commercial ventures and funding for the Mount Evans Corridor. These include concession operations in addition to transportation, food and beverage, infrastructure, retail, and other issues.

Partners

Many different agencies and organizations have vested interests in the Mount Evans Corridor. The USFS manages much of the mountain as part of the Arapaho and Roosevelt National Forests. The auto road to the top is managed and maintained by the Colorado Department of Transportation; the wilderness area is managed by the Colorado Department of Wildlife; The City of Denver Department of Parks and Recreation owns and manages a Denver Mountain Park at Echo Lake along the road to the summit; the University of Denver manages an observatory near the summit; and the Corridor is located in Clear Creek County and near Idaho Springs, whose residents consider the area a local park. Other commercial and nonprofit groups also demand input into any decision-making process. Other groups formally included in the planning process are:

- Clear Creek Ranger District, United States Forest Service
- Colorado Natural Areas Program
- Colorado State University
- Denver Botanic Gardens
- Idaho Springs Chamber of Commerce
- Bicycle Colorado
- Colorado Natural Heritage Program
- University of Denver (USFS 1993)

Planning Issues and Alternatives

Management alternatives need to be environmentally sound solutions to meet the expected increase in use of the Byway in the future. These alternatives should note that within a five-year time frame all traffic in the Corridor needs to be regulated, and alternative forms of transportation need to be offered. Methods need to be developed to measure Corridor capacity for all modes of transportation. A training program for all commercial users, requiring a skilled interpreter to accompany all trips and offer written and oral interpretation to all visitors, should be developed. Finally, a plan of implementation for a reservation system for peak day use and a data collection system to survey all user experiences and evaluate management effectiveness should be considered. The following specific issues need to be examined:

- Facilities
- Preservation and protection
- Operation, administration, and funding sources
- Transportation issues
- Concessions
- Potential problems

What's Next?

The planning team for the Mount Evans Scenic Byway must strive to eliminate the problems faced by the Byway and focus on achievement of the stated goals and objectives. The area is very popular with the Font Range residents of Colorado and is a regular weekend and summer outing for many. In addition, many tourists who drive through Colorado in the summer months take advantage of the many attractions of the mountain. The real issues that are being considered are access, control, and management responsibility for the Byway.

Summary

Discussions among partner groups and interagency agreements will determine the sustainable development for the Mount Evans Scenic Byway. The USFS will not give up control of the National Forests, nor will the other agencies give up management of their turf. Clearly, the survival of the area is in the best interest of the visiting public and the local community. Before any final decisions are made, input will be solicited from all areas.

There are models for large conglomerates to manage natural areas successfully and provide stability for sustainable development and ultimately preservation of the environment. As an example, Aramark currently manages multiple national park sites, providing a cross-section of services while maintaining a good partnership relationship with the park management officials. This is only one example of the private sector operating in natural areas; other models should be sought out and studied.

Questions

1. How will existing facilities be maintained?
2. How practical would it be to pool resources?
3. Explain the impact of allowing individuals to drive to the top of the mountain, paying a fee, and limiting the number of visitors?
4. How will the issues in question 3 be resolved?
5. What private ventures are to be developed?
6. What are the existing operating models for development?

References

United States Forest Service. 1993. *Guiding principles.* Lakewood, Colo.: USFS promotional materials, Regional Office.

Wong, R. 1993. *Letter to planning team.* District Ranger, United States Forest Service.

Border Tourism Synergies in the North Country

New York and Quebec

Objectives

At the completion of this case study, students should be able to:

1. Identify a destination's tourism resources and compile the data into a logical format.
2. Select the key tourism tactics and strategies for a rural area to utilize in the tourism development process.
3. Assess a tourism resource base.

Case Study Narrative

Focus on tourism as a business and economic tool in the North Country of New York and the Province of Quebec is critical. Quebec has long been a tourism destination, and Montreal, the largest city in Quebec, attracts numerous visitors from around the world. The North Country of New York could benefit from this success—not by competing, but by complementing the attractions north of the border and enhancing its own offerings. The North Country of New York typically refers to the area of New York state north of Saratoga Springs and includes the Adirondack Park and the shores of Lake Champlain, places that have great potential for further tourism. Quebec Province and its attractions are well known for ski resorts, such as Mt. Tremblant; Montreal and its cosmopolitan and cultural attractions; and Quebec City, the seat of government for the province. Tourism in the North Country of New York is not as well developed, but there is great potential to partner with Quebec to market the entire border region effectively.

110

Numerous activities and events could be promoted in the border regions of Quebec and New York, including shopping; outdoor activities; visiting museums, historic sites, beaches, and national and state parks; attending cultural events and festivals; visiting theme and amusement parks; enjoying nightlife and dancing; gambling; attending sporting events; and engaging in sports such as golf, tennis, and skiing. The North Country of New York and southern Quebec, the border region, could benefit from a concerted effort and a formal partnership for tourism that might focus on some of the activities just listed. Many residents of the border region want the economic prosperity that growth and development bring, but not at the cost of a good quality of life. A slower pace and rural residential experience may have drawn people to the North Country, and these attributes can be balanced with tourism. Economic development for tourism must balance visitation and the quality-of-life issues that are important to local residents.

Good tourism does not just happen. It is planned and delivered in a strategic manner. The theory of "Build it and they will come" is not a sound strategy. In the initial stages of planning for tourism, a region or community such as the border region—and especially the North Country—must conduct a self-assessment. Self-assessment should act as a baseline for decision making (Deale/O'Halloran and Stynes 1987). Assessment categories for the North Country are listed in Table 1.

Tourism Planning Pilot Study

Preliminary research is also required to plan for tourism development. A survey was completed by students at the State University of New York (SUNY) Plattsburgh campus providing some initial insights into tourism in the North Country. The student group has some limitations, but respondents were from diverse geographic origins and were a mix of potential visitors to the area. The students had the following profile:

- 83 percent were 18–25 years of age
- 7 percent were 26–33 years of age
- 3 percent were 34–41 years of age
- 1 percent were 40–49 years of age
- 1 percent were age 50 and over
- 30 males and 55 females
- 79 percent full-time students
- 85 percent New York residents
- 6 percent from other states, including Arizona, Illinois, Vermont, and Wisconsin
- 9 percent from other countries, including Canada, the Dominican Republic, England, Japan, Korea, and Singapore

Students were asked to name their most common leisure activity. Respondents indicated that camping was the most popular activity, and swimming and

Table 1 North Country Tourism Resources

Tourism Resources	Strength	Weakness	Opportunity	Threat
Natural Resources				
New York				
Climate: seasons	Fall, Summer	Winters harsh	Winter sports	TBD
Water resources: lakes, streams, waterfalls	Lake Champlain, Au Sable River	Limited access and launches	Sports development	Pollution Nonindigenous species
Flora: forests, flowers, shrubs, wild edibles	Adirondacks, Thickly wooded forests	Limited access Lack of staging areas Limited data distribution	Sustainable development, visitor ethics, staging information centers	Pollution Overuse
Fauna: fish and wildlife	Deer, moose, salmon, trout, bass	Population control	Recreation development	Pollution
Geological resources: topography, soils, beaches, dunes, rocks and minerals, fossils	Au Sable Chasm, Lake Champlain beaches	Limited access	Tourism access, development Camping, hiking	Sustainable use
Scenery: combinations of all of the above	Autumn foliage, Mountain views	Competitiveness	Can be competitive	Lack of promotion and awareness
Physical location	Proximity to Montreal, Burlington, VT Winter sports center in Lake Placid	Remote from population centers	Partnership with Quebec tourism	Distance from U.S. population centers Gas prices, etc.
Province of Quebec	St. Lawrence Seaway, mountains, wooded areas	Harsh winters	Year round use in place	Competing for tourism dollars
Cultural Resources				
New York				
Historic buildings and sites	Kent Delord, AFB Oval, McDonough Monument, Champlain Monument	Nondevelopment, maintenance	Battle of Plattsburgh Historic Museum	Lack of funds for development
Cuisine	The Michigan	Little for which the North Country is known	French Canadian food, game food Michigans, maple sugar	Lack of promotion and awareness

112

Ethnic cultures	Proximity to Native American attractions, rich history, French Canadian heritage	Perceived limited cultural diversity	Tie to cultural heritage Native Americans, Quebec: French Canadian Heritage *Jamaican	Lack of cohesive ethnic communities
Industry, government, religion	Interested and willing	Limited local funding	Redevelopment of old base in Plattsburgh	Lack of infrastructure
Anthropological resources	TBD	TBD	TBD	TBD
Local celebrities	TBD	TBD	TBD	TBD
Province of Quebec	Has it all	Some guests presume language is an issue	Promotion	TBD
Human Resources **New York**				
Hospitality skills	SUNY Plattsburgh, Paul Smiths	Community acceptance of tourism	Training	Training
Management skills	SUNY, Paul Smiths	Diverse	Training, Seasonal labor force	Training
Performing artists: music, drama, art, storytellers	University cultural events	TBD	TBD	TBD
Local universities and colleges	Community theatre			
Craftsmen and artisans	Unique Adirondack style	TBD	Incorporate crafts and arts in existing festivals	TBD
Other labor skills from chefs to lawyers	TBD	Blue collar to white collar	Retraining	Funds for retraining

Province of Quebec	Population is strong	TBD	Language immersion	TBD
Capital **New York**				
Availability of capital	Local officials embrace tourism development ideas	Limited community support	Marketing and education about tourism	Lack of community support
Infrastructure: transportation; drive locations, discussion of regular	Move Plattsburgh Airport to Air Force base	Time lag in airport opening Drive to remote location	Speed of process Development of train service to and from Montreal and southern New York	Major tenant
Harbors and marinas, trails and walkways	Expand harbor development in Plattsburgh	TBD	TBD	TBD
Infrastructure Utilities	Low electrical cost	Limited number of Internet connections	TBD	Renegotiation of electricity contract with Quebec Hydro
Water, power, waste treatment, communications	Plentiful water	Water treatment plant on the waterfront in downtown Plattsburgh	TBD	TBD
Province of Quebec	Relatively strong economy	(9/11 comeback still in place)	TBD: joint research with the North Country	TBD

Note: TBD: To be determined

hiking were also popular. Table 2 indicates the leisure activities participated in by the respondents. Many respondents engaged in outdoor recreation and sports activities. A variety of other activities with varying rates of participation, including snowboarding, skating, maple sugaring, and canoeing, were mentioned.

Image Questions. Several image questions were also presented on the survey. The first question concerning images, asked of the respondents presently living in the area was, "What was your image of this area before coming here?" Answers were varied, including discussions of climate, that it is of small to medium size, that there is not much to do, and that it is a mountain area, an area with outdoor recreation, characterized by farmlands and fields, a college town, close to Montreal, beautiful, quiet, historical, and has a low crime rate.

The second image question on the survey was, "What is your image of this area now that you live here?" Again, the answers varied. Responses included that the area is beautiful, peaceful, too windy, too cold, snowy, underdeveloped, full of winter sports, rural, known for its outdoor environment, and has expanded business growth.

When asked what destination comes to mind when one thinks of tourism in the North Country, the most frequent answer was Lake Placid. Lake Champlain ranked second, with Whiteface Ski Area ranked third. Others stated the entire Adirondack region as a destination, which was not very specific. Of more interest was that several respondents chose Montreal as a destination and it is not part of the North Country of New York at all. The results were not surprising; many people are perhaps aware of Lake Placid because of the past Olympics. Furthermore, the North

Table 2   Leisure Activity Participation

Activity	Number	Percent
Hiking	42	44%
Bicycling	28	29
Fishing	26	27
Ice fishing	12	13
Snowshoeing	6	6
Downhill skiing	28	29
Cross-country skiing	8	8
Kayaking	8	8
Whitewater rafting	13	14
Boating	25	26
Sailing	5	5
Swimming	41	43
Camping	48	51
Hunting	10	11

Source: Deale et al. 2002.

Country holds a lot of just that, *country,* not to mention smaller towns that are not necessarily focused on tourism.

There were sixteen different answers to the question, "What tourism destinations have you visited in the North Country?" The most popular answer was Lake Placid with six responses. Right behind Lake Placid, with five responses, was Lake Champlain. Ausable Chasm and the Adirondacks were the next most popular destinations with three responses.

Those surveyed were asked to rate shopping, entertainment, transportation, outdoor recreation, dining, and lodging in the North Country. The rating scale was 1 (poor) through 5 (excellent). The results, calculated as an average, were: outdoor recreation, 3.68; lodging, 3.17; transportation, 2.67; dining, 2.67; entertainment, 2.3; and shopping, 2.11. It can be concluded that the respondents believed that the North Country, especially Plattsburgh, lacked shopping places.

Respondents were also asked, "What type(s) of tourist attractions could or should be developed to attract visitors to this area? (Please check all that apply.)" The types of tourism attractions that respondents believed should be developed included:

Entertainment	58 people (15%)
Festivals	54 people (14%)
Lake development	47 people (12%)
Lake Champlain boat tours	47 people (12%)
Amusements	43 people (11%)
Trails	33 people (9%)
Historic attractions	30 people (8%)
The arts	30 people (8%)
Museums	19 people (5%)
Conventions	19 people (5%)

The information gathered points out the need for the area to further develop its sense of place. As a famous tourism planner Clare Gunn (1994) stated, "The greatest imperative for all of tourism is place." Sometimes in this modern era there seems to be a push to homogenize the world, and yet for the sake of tourism and healthy communities the unique qualities of a place are essential. The North Country of New York would do well to further develop a sense of place throughout its communities and natural resource areas to benefit tourism and its residents (Deale et al. 2002). Analysis of these results by experts has suggested that tourism development for the North Country could focus on:

• Preserving natural areas: Flora, fauna, geologic features, lake shores
• Native American / First Nation tourism: Culture and heritage
• Food tourism: Regional specialties, wild game foods

Challenges and Issues for the Future

The North Country already has the beginning of a partnership with Quebec. In an effort to establish a heritage trail along the length of Lake Champlain, organizers have held meetings with local residents in New York, Quebec, and Vermont.

It is paramount that North Country tourism industry professionals speak with one voice so that the perceptions and meaning of tourism are clear. Trends such as adventure travel, biking vacations, increased family travel (including business travelers taking their children with them), cultural and historic tourism, green travel, gaming, travel utilizing the Internet, and increased minority travel will all alter the current services available to the traveling public (TIA 2002). All these opportunities could be leveraged in the North Country through natural areas, entertainment (e.g., casinos), and the enhancement of cultural attractions and special events.

North Country tourism is a business that can change the face of the region, and the next generation of leaders will help shape its future through professionalism, critical thinking, and sound decision making. Border synergies between Quebec and the North Country to help promote tourism make sense, and while Quebec has cultivated tourism extensively, the North Country has many opportunities to advance its tourism efforts; both areas will reap the benefits.

Questions

1. What do the data from the tourism assessment and the data from the pilot study suggest for tourism development in the North Country?
2. Are the themes of natural preservation, Native American, First Nation tourism, and food tourism consistent with the data results?
3. What would be a suggested strategy for tourism development in the North Country?

References

Deale, C. et al. 2002. Tourism images of the north country of New York: A pilot study as a class project. In T. Damonte. (ed.). *Proceedings for the annual conference of the southeastern council of hotel, restaurant, and tourism education,* November, Myrtle Beach, S.C.

Deale, C., O'Halloran, R., and D. Stynes. 1987. *Tourism Planning,* Tourism Information Series No. 2. Cooperative Extension Service. Michigan State University, Extension Bulletin E–2004.

Gunn, C. 1994. *Tourism planning: Basics, concepts, cases.* Philadelphia: Taylor & Francis.

Travel Industry Association of America (TIA). 2002. *Travel statistics and trends.* Retrieved December 4, 2002, from http://www.tia.org.